SOUP MAKER RECIPE

1200 Days of Easy & Delicious Recipes for Every Day Meals Suitable For All Soup Machines, Blenders & Kettles Ready in Less Than 30 Mins

Poula Ray

Table of Contents

1. Introduction

A soup maker cookbook is a great way to change unhealthy eating habits. These cookbooks are filled with a variety of soup recipes that are healthy and tasty. They also offer various cooking methods, so that you can create many types of meals using your machine. In addition to recipes, soup maker cookbooks also offer health benefits.

Recipes

You can create delicious soups with a soup maker machine by using the right recipes. The process is easy and you only need a few ingredients. The machine does all the hard work! The recipes are flexible enough to use with any type of cooking appliance. The recipes are also easy to make and can be modified to suit your cooking style.

Buying a soup maker cookbook

Soup maker cookbooks are available in paperback and digital format and can be used to cook a variety of different soups and stews. They contain information on the cooking process and ingredients used, as well as measurements that will work in the UK. However, buying a cookbook doesn't make you an expert in soup-making. You will still need to learn about different ingredients and cooking techniques to get the best results.

A soup maker can help you save time and effort by reducing the number of steps involved in preparing a soup.

Chapter 1:   Tips on How to Use the Soup Maker

One of the benefits of a soup maker is the convenience it offers. A soup maker can be easily cleaned and used to cook soup or other meals on the go. The size of a serving depends on who will be eating it and where you live. A small jug of soup will likely be more than enough for a single adult, but if you're cooking for a family or group, you may want to consider buying a larger jug.

Easy to use

An easy to use soup maker is a kitchen appliance that can help you make delicious soups in minutes. Its stainless steel body gives it a classic look, and its inner body is easy to clean. It also has a variety of preset programs so you can cook the type of soup you want without too much work.

A good soup maker has 4 preset programs and a blender function to tailor the consistency of the soup. You can easily prep the ingredients for your soup by chopping them and placing them in the soup maker. The LCD display tells you when your soup is ready and how long it will take. It is easy to clean and has a dishwasher-safe bowl.

One model is the Instant Pot, which has a memory function that allows you to adjust seasoning and add extra ingredients as the soup cooks. Plus, unlike other soup makers, you can taste your soup while it's cooking to ensure that it's just right. The Instant Pot also allows you to keep your soup warm for up to two hours.

Easy to clean

If you have a soup maker, it's important to clean it as soon as possible after each use. Rinsing and wiping down with warm soapy water will make cleanup much easier. This method will also ensure that the soup maker doesn't have too much residue left behind. To keep your soup maker as clean as possible, you can clean it using warm soapy water and a soft cloth.

The Total Control model has a removable inner pot and a Pre-Clean function that ensures the unit stays super clean. It also comes with an in-built pause function that allows you to make tweaks in the middle of the cooking process. This model also allows you to reheat soup in two, three, or four portions, which means less washing up. If you need to reheat soup after the first cooking, you can use the reheating function to keep the soup warm.

The Philips soup maker is an elegant stainless steel option. It has a 1.2-liter capacity and can produce fresh soup in 18-20 minutes. It has a unique blade design and operates on 120 volts. It has six preset programs, including pureed soup, chunky soup, smoothies, and milk-based soup.

Adapting recipes for soup makers

Many soup makers use a different cooking process than a regular pan. You may wonder how to adapt a recipe to work in a soup maker. The process depends on the type of soup maker you have, the ingredients used, and your personal preferences. Here are some suggestions for cooking in a soup maker.

First, learn the basics of a soup maker's functions. A good soup maker will come with a user manual and recipes. You can consult these documents whenever you encounter difficulties. You can also contact the manufacturer for technical support. The user manual will detail the main principles of how to use the soup maker and what ingredients and stocks to use. It will also describe how to use different models.

Another important tip for making soup in a soup maker is to use enough liquid. The amount of liquid you add will determine how thick the finished product is. Most soup makers recommend 750ml of liquid per batch. To prevent burning, be sure that the ingredients are evenly distributed. Also, make sure that the ingredients don't touch the bottom of the machine.

Cleaning a soup maker

Cleaning a soup maker is easy if you follow a few simple steps. First, rinse out the pot with warm water and soap. Next, wipe the pot with a soft cloth. Rinsing the soup maker will leave less residue to clean, which will make clean-up easier. It's also a good idea to add water to the pot while cleaning to avoid food sticking to the pot.

If the soup maker is burnt, use water and a cleaning solution that contains baking soda or biological washing powder. Scrub until there is no trace of food or residue remaining on the bottom. When finished, rinse the soup maker thoroughly and place it in the fridge to dry. It's best to wait at least eight hours before using the soup maker again.

Kettle soup makers often resemble milkshake machines. This type of soup maker is great for making a small amount of soup at a time. However, it's important not to overfill it, as this will break it. Kettle soup makers are more delicate than most other soup makers, so take extra care to clean them.

Chapter 2: Breakfast Recipes

Recipe 1: Asparagus and Potato Soup

Serving Size: 4

Cooking Time: 30 minutes

Ingredients:

- 1 large potato, peeled, diced
- 600g asparagus, peeled, chopped
- 2 chicken bouillon cubes
- 250ml whipped cream
- Sugar, to taste
- Chopped spring onions, for garnish
- 750ml boiling water

Directions:

1. In the soup maker, add boiling water and chicken bouillon cubes. Stir to dissolve bouillon cubes
2. Add potatoes, asparagus and sugar. Be sure not to overfill your machine.
3. Close the lid and cook on smooth. Once your soup maker cycle is done, mix egg yolk and cream in a bowl and stir into the soup.
4. Close the lid and select blend function.

Nutritional Value: Calories 175; Fat 9g; Carbohydrates 15g; Protein 9g

Recipe 2: Bacon Broccoli Soup

Serving Size: 4

Cooking Time: 25 minutes

Ingredients:

- 650ml chicken stock
- 2 heads broccoli, chopped
- 4 bacon rashers, sliced
- 1 potato, peeled, diced
- 1 onion, peeled, chopped
- 1 celery sticks, chopped
- Salt, to taste
- Freshly ground black pepper, to taste

Directions:

1. Heat a small nonstick saucepan over medium-high.
2. Add onions, garlic, and bacon. Cook and stir for 3 minutes. Transfer the mixture into the Soup Maker. If your Soup Maker has the sauté function, cook the bacon, onions, and garlic in it.
3. Add all remaining prepared ingredients and close the lid. Set on smooth.
4. Your soup will be ready in 20 to 25 minutes.
5. Serve immediately and enjoy.

Nutritional Value: Calories 217; Fat 0g; Carbohydrates 41g; Protein 10g

Recipe 3: Bacon Sweet Potato Soup

Serving Size: 4

Cooking Time: 30 minutes

Ingredients:

- 4 chopped bacon slices
- 3 sweet potatoes, peeled, diced
- 750ml chicken stock
- 1 lime, juiced
- 1 red onion, peeled, diced
- 2 crushed garlic cloves
- Salt and pepper, to taste

Directions:

1. Add all ingredients into the soup maker except bacon. Be sure not to overfill. Close the lid and cook on smooth function.
2. Once the soup maker cycle is complete, adjust seasoning and serve soup with bacon.

Nutritional Value: Calories 146; Fat 8g; Carbohydrates 21g; Protein 2g

Recipe 4: Blended Broccoli Soup

Serving Size: 4

Cooking Time: 30 minutes

Ingredients:

- ½ courgette
- 1 small, peeled onion
- 1 teaspoon of thyme
- 2 tablespoons of Greek yoghurt
- 1 medium head of broccoli
- 1 teaspoon of oregano
- 468ml / 15.8oz water
- Salt and pepper

Directions:

1. Chop up the courgette and broccoli and add to soup maker
2. Add the water and season
3. Cook using the blend function for 25 minutes
4. Add the Greek yoghurt and stir thoroughly
5. Serve and enjoy.

Nutritional Value: Calories 70; Fat 0g; Carbohydrates 13g; Protein 5g

Recipe 5: Broccoli Dill Soup

Serving Size: 5

Cooking Time: 30 minutes

Ingredients:

- 2 sprigs dill, fresh
- 1 head broccoli, cut into florets
- 1 chicken stock cube
- Fresh mixed herbs, to taste
- 1.2 liters boiling water

Directions:

1. Add boiling water and stock cube into the soup maker. Stir to dissolve stock cubes
2. Add broccoli, dill, herbs, salt and pepper. Be sure not to overfill your soup maker.
3. Close the lid and cook on smooth setting.
4. Once the soup maker cycle is complete, serve topped with cream and cheese.

Nutritional Value: Calories 160; Fat 11g; Carbohydrates 10.4g; Protein 7.6g

Recipe 6: Carrot and Coriander Soup

Serving Size: 2

Cooking Time: 28 minutes

Ingredients:

- 16 medium carrots, peeled, diced
- 4 tablespoons coriander, fresh, chopped
- 1 teaspoon garlic puree
- 1 pinch nutmeg
- 1 onion, peeled, diced
- 15ml lemon juice
- 200ml hot vegetable stock

Directions:

1. In the Soup Maker, add all ingredients, close the lid, set on blend function, and let it cook for 25 minutes or according to your Soup Maker setting.
2. Serve and enjoy!

Nutritional Value: Calories 130; Fat 7g; Carbohydrates 13g; Protein 5g

Recipe 7: Cauliflower and Roquefort Cheese Soup

Serving Size: 4

Cooking Time: 40 minutes

Ingredients:

- 1 tablespoon olive oil
- 1 onion, chopped
- 750ml/3 cups vegetable stock
- 1 stick celery, chopped
- 1 leek, chopped
- 125g/4oz potatoes, peeled & cubed
- 1 bay leaf (remove before blending)
- 450g/1lb cauliflower florets
- 120ml/½ cup low fat cream
- 50g/2oz Roquefort cheese (or vegetarian alternative)
- 2 tablespoon freshly chopped chives
- Salt & pepper to taste

Directions:

1. Add all the prepared ingredients to the soup maker except the cream and chives. Cover and leave to actually cook on high for 30 minutes.
2. Ensure all the ingredients are well combined, tender and piping hot. Remove the bay leaf and blend to your preferred consistency (or leave your machine to do this as programmed).
3. Stir through the cream and leave to warm through for a minute or two. Adjust the seasoning and serve with the chopped chives sprinkled on top.

Nutritional Value: Calories 146; Fat 8g; Carbohydrates 21g; Protein 2g

Recipe 8: Cheeky Chicken Soup

Serving Size: 2

Cooking Time: 35 minutes

Ingredients:

- 1 chopped onion
- 1 chopped large carrot
- 700ml / 23.7oz of chicken stock
- 150g / 5.3oz of skinless, shredded roast chicken
- 100g / 3.5oz frozen peas
- 1 ½ tablespoons of Greek yoghurt
- ½ small, crushed garlic clove
- Squeeze of lemon juice

Directions:

1. Add the carrots, onion, and peas to your soup maker
2. Choose the chunky soup program
3. Once the program ends stir in the chicken and leave to warm
4. Mix the garlic, yoghurt, and lemon juice together
5. Season and pour into bowls, add the rest of the yoghurt, and serve.

Nutritional Value: Calories 155; Fat 5g; Carbohydrates 8g; Protein 17g

Recipe 9: Chicken and Potato Soup

Serving Size: 4

Cooking Time: 30 minutes

Ingredients:

- 1 liter hot chicken stock
- 200g chicken, cooked, cut into shreds
- 200g potatoes, peeled, chopped
- 1 onion, peeled, chopped
- 2 garlic cloves, minced

Directions:

1. In the soup maker, add potatoes, onions, garlic, chicken, and chicken stock. Be sure not to overfill your soup maker.
2. Close the lid and cook on smooth setting.

Nutritional Value: Calories 235; Fat 9g; Carbohydrates 12g; Protein 6g

Recipe 10: Clearly Skinny Celery Soup

Serving Size: 4

Cooking Time: 30 minutes

Ingredients:

- 6 sticks of celery
- 1 peeled onion
- 4 peeled carrots
- 250ml / 8.5oz water
- 2 tablespoons of cream cheese
- 1 teaspoon of chives
- 1 teaspoon of mixed herbs
- Salt and pepper

Directions:

1. Chop the celery into pieces of 1cm and put into your soup maker
2. Dice the prepared carrots and onion and add to the soup maker
3. Add the seasoning and water then cook on the blend function for 25 minutes
4. Add the cream cheese to thicken, blend and serve.

Nutritional Value: Calories 76; Fat 3g; Carbohydrates 10g; Protein 4g

Recipe 11: Cream of Crab Soup

Serving Size: 4

Cooking Time: 25 minutes

Ingredients:

- Knob of butter
- ½ onion, peeled and chopped
- 250ml/1 cup chicken stock/broth
- ¼ teaspoon celery salt
- 1 dash freshly ground black pepper
- 750ml/3 cups milk
- 450g/1lb crabmeat, cooked and shredded
- Chopped fresh parsley to garnish

Directions:

1. Add all the ingredients, except the crabmeat and parsley, to the soup maker. Cover and leave to actually cook on high for 20 minutes.
2. Fold in the crabmeat and leave to warm through for a further 3-5 minutes. Ensure all the ingredients are well combined, tender and piping hot.
3. Blend to your preferred consistency (or leave your machine to do this as programmed). Adjust the seasoning and serve, garnished with parsley.

Nutritional Value: Calories 160; Fat 11g; Carbohydrates 10.4g; Protein 7.6g

Recipe 12: Creamy Cullen Skink Soup

Serving Size: 4

Cooking Time: 32 minutes

Ingredients:

- 450 g. haddock, smoked fillets, diced
- 600 ml milk
- 2 celery stalks, sliced
- 1 bay leaf
- 1 onion, diced
- 2 medium potatoes, peeled, cooked mashed
- 56 g. butter
- Pepper
- Salt
- Parsley (a handful, for garnish)

Directions:

1. Transfer all your ingredients, except the bay leaf to the soup maker and stir well.
2. Seal soup maker with lid and cook on smooth mode.
3. When done, switch off the Soup Maker, add in bay leaf, and cover. Allow bay leaf to be infused for about 5 minutes.
4. Discard bay leaf. Season soup with salt and pepper. Serve and enjoy.

Nutritional Value: Calories 213; Fat 10g; Carbohydrates 30g; Protein 26g

Recipe 13: Garlic, Bacon and Cannellini Soup

Serving Size: 4

Cooking Time: 20 minutes

Ingredients:

- 1 tablespoon olive oil
- 125g/4oz lean back bacon, chopped
- 4 garlic cloves, crushed
- 1 onion chopped
- 1 carrot, chopped
- 1 celery stalk, chopped
- 3 tablespoon tomato puree/paste
- 500ml/2 cups vegetable stock
- 200ml/7oz tinned chopped tomatoes
- 200g/7oz tinned cannellini beans, drained
- 1 teaspoon each dried thyme & oregano
- Salt & pepper to taste

Directions:

1. Add all the prepared ingredients to the soup maker. Cover and leave to actually cook on high for 20 minutes. Ensure all the ingredients are well combined, tender and piping hot.
2. Blend to your preferred consistency (or leave your machine to do this as programmed). Adjust the seasoning and serve.

Nutritional Value: Calories 197; Fat 10g; Carbohydrates 13g; Protein 13g

Recipe 14: Ginger Carrot Soup

Serving Size: 4

Cooking Time: 30 minutes

Ingredients:

- 600g carrot, chopped
- 3 tablespoons gingerroot, fresh, grated
- 700ml vegetable stock
- 2 garlic clove, minced
- 1 medium onion, chopped
- Salt and pepper, to taste
- 1 tablespoon olive oil

Directions:

1. Using the sauté function, sauté onions in hot oil for 3 minutes, add garlic and cook for 1 minute. Mix in carrots and ginger. Cook for another 2 minutes.
2. Add all remaining ingredients. Close the lid and cook for 21 minutes.

Nutritional Value: Calories 130; Fat 7g; Carbohydrates 13g; Protein 5g

Recipe 15: Ham and Pea Soup

Serving Size: 4

Cooking Time: 35 minutes

Ingredients:

- 300g ham, cooked, chopped
- 500g peas, frozen
- 1 Liter boiling water
- 2 pork stock cubes
- 1 sweet potato, peeled, cut into cubes
- 1 onion, chopped
- 1 teaspoon butter

Directions:

1. Set your Soup Maker to sauté mode. Add butter. When melted, cook onions until tender, about 5 minutes.
2. Add stock cubes and boiling water, stir to dissolve.
3. Add all remaining ingredients.
4. Close the lid, set on smooth, and cook for 30 minutes.

Nutritional Value: Calories 235; Fat 9g; Carbohydrates 12g; Protein 6g

Recipe 16: Lemon and Avocado Soup

Serving Size: 4

Cooking Time: 20 minutes

Ingredients:

- 1 teaspoon olive oil
- 2 teaspoon lemon juice
- 1 onion, chopped
- 500ml/2 cups vegetable stock
- 2 ripe avocadoes, flesh scooped out
- 1 large cucumber, peeled & chopped
- 60ml/ ¼ cup whole milk
- 60ml/ ¼ cup skimmed milk
- 1 vine ripened tomato, chopped
- Salt & pepper to taste

Directions:

1. Add all the prepared ingredients to the soup maker, except the chopped tomato and half the chopped cucumber. Cover and leave to actually cook on high for 10 minutes. Ensure all the ingredients are well combined, tender and piping hot.
2. Blend to your preferred consistency (or leave your machine to do this as programmed). Leave to cool. Chill, adjust the seasoning and serve with the reserved chopped tomatoes and cucumber sprinkled over each bowl.

Nutritional Value: Calories 181; Fat 13g; Carbohydrates 34g; Protein 16g

Recipe 17: Mushroom and Tomato Soup

Serving Size: 4

Cooking Time: 30 minutes

Ingredients:

- 400g mushrooms, sliced
- 3 tomatoes, cut into quarters
- 2 red onions, sliced
- 350g potatoes, peeled, diced
- 1 pinch mixed herbs
- 1 pinch fresh ground pepper
- 1 teaspoon salt
- 1 vegetable stock cube
- 500ml hot water

Directions:

1. In the Soup Maker, dissolve vegetable stock cube in hot water and add all remaining ingredients.
2. Put the lid on and choose smooth function.
3. Wait for the cycle to complete and enjoy!

Nutritional Value: Calories 197; Fat 10g; Carbohydrates 13g; Protein 13g

Recipe 18: Pea and Asparagus Soup

Serving Size: 4

Cooking Time: 30 minutes

Ingredients:

- 1 cup peas, frozen
- 3 ounces asparagus, trimmed, chopped
- 1 leek, white part chopped
- 1tablespon dill, chopped
- 2 tablespoons olive oil
- 1 teaspoon lemon rind, grated
- 750ml hot vegetable stock
- Salt, to taste
- Fresh ground black pepper, to taste

Directions:

1. If your Soup Maker has the sauté function, turn it on, if not use a skillet for this step.
2. Add oil and once hot, cook asparagus and leek for 3 minutes.
3. Add dill, lemon rind, peas, vegetable stock, and season with salt and pepper.
4. Put the lid on and press the smooth function.
5. You may now wait for your soup to cook.

Nutritional Value: Calories 226; Fat 8g; Carbohydrates 34g; Protein 9g

Recipe 19: Pea and Leek Soup

Serving Size: 4

Cooking Time: 30 minutes

Ingredients:

- 1 tablespoon olive oil
- 1 medium leek, sliced
- 1 clove garlic, peeled and chopped
- 1 medium potato, peeled and chopped
- 750ml/3 cups vegetable stock/broth
- 450g/1lb frozen peas
- Salt and pepper
- 1 Little Gem lettuce, shredded

Directions:

1. Add all the ingredients, except the lettuce, to the soup maker. Cover and leave to actually cook on high for 30 minutes. Ensure all the ingredients are well combined, tender and piping hot.
2. Blend to your preferred consistency (or leave your machine to do this as programmed). Add the shredded lettuce, adjust the seasoning and serve.

Nutritional Value: Calories 138; Fat 9g; Carbohydrates 14g; Protein 8.4g

Recipe 20: Pepper Mushroom Soup

Serving Size: 4

Cooking Time: 30 minutes

Ingredients:

- 1 liter hot beef stock
- 400g mushrooms, chopped
- 1 ½ teaspoons ground peppercorns
- 1 onion, peeled, chopped
- 1 leek, chopped

Directions:

1. Add all prepared ingredients into the soup maker and close the lid. Be sure not to overfill your soup maker.
2. Cook on smooth setting.

Nutritional Value: Calories 260; Fat 21g; Carbohydrates 9g; Protein 12g

Recipe 21: Peppery Vegetable Soup

Serving Size: 4

Cooking Time: 21 minutes

Ingredients:

- 3 red peppers, seeds removed, sliced
- 2 garlic cloves, minced
- 2 potatoes, peeled, diced
- 1 teaspoon chilli powder
- 2 small onions, diced
- 1 Liter hot vegetable stock
- 2 teaspoons paprika
- Salt and pepper, to taste

Directions:

1. Add all ingredients into your Soup Maker.
2. Close the lid and cook for 21 minutes on smooth setting.
3. Taste and season with salt and pepper.

Nutritional Value: Calories 176; Fat 11g; Carbohydrates 20g; Protein 6g

Recipe 22: Potato and Bacon Soup

Serving Size: 8

Cooking Time: 40 minutes

Ingredients:

- 1 tablespoon olive oil
- 5 slices back bacon
- 1 medium onion, peeled and chopped
- 3 cloves garlic, crushed
- 6 medium potatoes, peeled and chopped
- 1lt/4 cups chicken stock
- 1½ teaspoon salt
- 1 teaspoon ground pepper
- 250ml/1 cup single cream
- 2 tablespoon mature cheddar cheese, grated, to garnish

Directions:

1. Fry the prepared bacon in a pan until crisp, and chop.
2. Add all the prepared ingredients to the soup maker except the cheese, cream and bacon. Cover and leave to actually cook on high for 40 minutes. Ensure all the ingredients are well combined, tender and piping hot. Blend to your preferred consistency (or leave your machine to do this as programmed). Adjust the seasoning and ladle into bowls.
3. Stir through the cream, top with the chopped bacon and some grated cheese.

Nutritional Value: Calories 217; Fat 0g; Carbohydrates 41g; Protein 10g

Recipe 23: Separated Salad Soup

Serving Size: 4

Cooking Time: 30 minutes

Ingredients:

- ¼ of white cabbage
- 1 red pepper
- 3 sticks of celery
- 1 teaspoon of oregano
- Salt and pepper
- 1 green pepper
- 4 carrots
- 2 tomatoes
- 100ml / 3.4oz water

Directions:

1. Deseed the peppers, peel the carrots and then chop all salad items
2. Add all ingredients to your soup maker
3. Cook for 25 minutes on the blend feature
4. Serve.

Nutritional Value: Calories 75; Fat 0g; Carbohydrates 16g; Protein 2g

Recipe 24: Spiced Butternut Squash and Carrot Soup

Serving Size: 4

Cooking Time: 30 minutes

Ingredients:

- ½ butternut squash, peeled, cubed
- 3 carrots, peeled, diced
- 1 red onion, peeled, diced
- 1 potato, peeled, diced
- 1 tablespoon dried coriander
- 1 tablespoon cumin seeds
- 1 tablespoon ginger, peeled, grated
- 1 red chili, seeds removed
- 500ml hot vegetable stock

Directions:

1. In the soup maker, add potatoes, carrots, onion, ginger, chili, cumin, coriander, and vegetable stock. Be sure not to overfill your soup maker
2. Close the lid and cook on smooth setting.
3. Once the soup maker cycle is done, adjust seasoning and serve.

Nutritional Value: Calories 226; Fat 8g; Carbohydrates 34g; Protein 9g

Recipe 25: Spiced Cauliflower Soup

Serving Size: 4

Cooking Time: 30 minutes

Ingredients:

- 400g cauliflower, cut into florets
- 800ml boiling water
- ½ teaspoon mixed spice
- ½ teaspoon paprika
- 3 vegetable stock cubes
- 200g potato, peeled, diced
- 1 onion, diced
- Sea salt, to taste
- Fresh ground black pepper, to taste

Directions:

1. In the soup maker, add all ingredients. Be sure not to overfill your soup maker.
2. Close the lid and cook on smooth function.
3. Once the soup maker cycle is done, adjust seasonings and serve.

Nutritional Value: Calories 199; Fat 13g; Carbohydrates 5g; Protein 16g

Recipe 26: Spicy Chicken and Egg Noodle Soup

Serving Size: 4

Cooking Time: 20 minutes

Ingredients:

- 1 tablespoon olive oil
- 450g/1lb skinless chicken breast, cubed
- 150g/5oz fine egg noodles
- 1 onion chopped
- 5 shallots, chopped
- 750ml/3 cups chicken stock
- 4 free range eggs, hardboiled, peeled & halved
- 1 tablespoon freshly grated ginger
- 1 teaspoon each ground coriander/cilantro, turmeric & crushed chilli flakes
- 1 tablespoon freshly chopped coriander/cilantro
- 2 stalks lemongrass, peeled & finely chopped
- 125g/4oz beansprouts
- 2 tablespoon lime juice
- Salt & pepper to taste

Directions:

1. Add all the prepared ingredients to the soup maker except the lime juice, bean sprouts and hard boiled eggs. Cover and leave to actually cook on high for 20 minutes.
2. Ensure all the ingredients are well combined, tender and piping hot. Adjust the seasoning, stir in the lime and serve with the bean sprouts and two egg halves on top.

Nutritional Value: Calories 215; Fat 6.6g; Carbohydrates 14g; Protein 26.6g

Recipe 27: Squash and Leek Soup

Serving Size: 4

Cooking Time: 25 minutes

Ingredients:

- 4 leeks, sliced
- 1 butternut squash, chopped
- 1 Liter boiling water
- 1 teaspoon chives
- 1 teaspoon garlic, ground
- 2 onions, sliced
- 3 tablespoons Greek yogurt
- Salt and pepper, to taste

Directions:

1. Add all ingredients into your machine with the exception of yogurt.
2. Close the lid and cook for 25 minutes on smooth setting.
3. Top each serving with a prepared dollop of yogurt.

Nutritional Value: Calories 130; Fat 7g; Carbohydrates 13g; Protein 5g

Recipe 28: Tomato and Cabbage Soup

Serving Size: 4

Cooking Time: 26 minutes

Ingredients:

- 340 g of cabbage, chopped
- 412 ml hot water
- 1 vegetable stock cube
- 400 g passata
- 1.64 g garlic, chopped
- 1 carrot, sliced
- 1 large onion, chopped
- 15 ml olive oil
- Pepper
- Salt

Directions:

1. Heat oil in a large-sized pan over medium heat. Add the prepared onion and garlic and sauté until onion is softened. Transfer to the soup maker. Add remaining ingredients to the soup maker and stir well.
2. Seal soup maker with lid and cook on smooth mode for 21 minutes. Season soup with salt and pepper.
3. Serve and enjoy.

Nutritional Value: Calories 108; Fat 4g; Carbohydrates 21g; Protein 3g

Recipe 29: Tomato, Saffron and Seafood Soup

Serving Size: 4

Cooking Time: 30 minutes

Ingredients:

- 1 tablespoon olive oil
- 3 garlic cloves, crushed
- 1 onion, chopped
- Half a fennel bulb, chopped
- 250g/9oz skinless, boneless turbot fillet, chopped
- 125g/4oz shelled cooked prawns
- Large pinch saffron threads
- ½ teaspoon crushed chilli flakes
- 750ml/3 cups chicken stock
- 1 fresh tomato, chopped
- 3 tablespoon each tomato puree/paste & freshly chopped flat leaf parsley
- Zest of 1 orange
- Salt & pepper to taste

Directions:

1. Add all the prepared ingredients to the soup maker, except the parsley. Cover and leave to actually cook on high for 30 minutes. Ensure all the ingredients are well combined, tender and piping hot.
2. Blend to your preferred consistency (or leave your machine to do this as programmed). Adjust the seasoning and serve with chopped parsley sprinkled over the top.

Nutritional Value: Calories 176; Fat 11g; Carbohydrates 20g; Protein 6g

Recipe 30: Vegetable and Bean Soup

Serving Size: 4

Cooking Time: 40 minutes

Ingredients:

- 360 g. white beans, rinsed
- 1 litre vegetable stock
- 3 garlic cloves, minced
- 2 celery stalks, diced
- 1 onion, chopped
- 0.23 g. dried thyme
- 4.2 g. sugar
- 1 bay leaf
- 2 oz. butter
- salt and pepper

Directions:

1. Melt butter in a prepared pan over medium heat. Add carrots, celery, and onion sauté until softened, about 5 minutes. Add garlic and sauté for a minute. Transfer to the soup maker.
2. Add remaining ingredients to the soup maker and stir well. Seal soup maker with lid and cook on chunky mode for 28 minutes.
3. Discard bay leaf. Serve and enjoy.

Nutritional Value: Calories 181; Fat 13g; Carbohydrates 34g; Protein 16g

Chapter 3: Lunch Recipes

Recipe 31: Aubergine and Butter Bean Soup

Serving Size: 4

Cooking Time: 30 minutes

Ingredients:

- 1 medium aubergine/eggplant, cubed
- 200g/7oz butter beans
- 750ml/3 cups vegetable stock/broth
- 120ml/½ cup cream
- Salt and pepper to taste

Directions:

1. Add all the prepared ingredients, except the cream, to the soup maker. Cover and leave to cook on high for 30 minutes. Ensure all the ingredients are well combined, tender and piping hot.
2. Blend to your preferred consistency (or leave your machine to do this as programmed). Stir in the cream and warm for a further minute. Adjust the seasoning and serve.

Nutritional Value: Calories 260; Fat 21g; Carbohydrates 9g; Protein 12g

Recipe 32: Beetroot Soup

Serving Size: 4

Cooking Time: 21 minutes

Ingredients:

- 600g beetroot, cooked, chopped
- 800ml hot vegetable stock
- 100g carrots, diced
- 100g red onions, chopped
- Salt and pepper, to taste

Directions:

1. Add beetroot, carrot, red onion, vegetable stock, and salt and pepper into your Soup Maker.
2. Close the lid and cook on smooth setting.

Nutritional Value: Calories 217; Fat 0g; Carbohydrates 41g; Protein 10g

Recipe 33: Bolognese Beef Soup

Serving Size: 4

Cooking Time: 21 minutes

Ingredients:

- 200g lean beef mince, cooked
- 400g tinned tomatoes, chopped
- 750ml beef stock
- 3 garlic cloves, minced
- 1 onion, chopped
- 2 tablespoons mixed herbs, dried
- 1 tablespoon olive oil

Directions:

1. In a small skillet, brown minced beef, drain and place in the Soup Maker.
2. Using the same skillet, sauté onions in hot olive oil and add to beef in the Soup Maker.
3. Add all remaining prepared ingredients and close the lid.
4. Choose smooth setting and wait for your soup to cook.

Nutritional Value: Calories 160; Fat 11g; Carbohydrates 10.4g; Protein 7.6g

Recipe 34: Cabbage Soup

Serving Size: 4

Cooking Time: 25 minutes

Ingredients:

- 500g cabbage, cut into shreds
- 800ml hot vegetable stock
- 100g onion, diced
- 100g potatoes, peeled, diced
- 1 garlic cloves, minced
- 1 teaspoon mixed herbs, fresh
- 1 teaspoon olive oil

Directions:

1. Heat oil in a prepared small skillet over medium heat. When hot, add prepared onions and cook for 3 minutes. Add garlic and herbs. Cook for 1 minute and transfer into the Soup Maker. If you Soup Maker has the sauté function, there is no need using an extra skillet.
2. Add potatoes, cabbage, and vegetable stock.
3. Close the lid and set on smooth. Leave it to cook for 20 to 25 minutes.
4. Taste and season as desired.

Nutritional Value: Calories 235; Fat 9g; Carbohydrates 12g; Protein 6g

Recipe 35: Carrot and Swede Soup

Serving Size: 4

Cooking Time: 30 minutes

Ingredients:

- 10 baby carrots, peeled, diced
- 1 swede, peeled, diced
- 2 tablespoons parsley
- 3 tablespoons sage
- 1 teaspoon garlic puree
- 1 liter hot vegetable stock
- Salt, to taste
- Fresh ground black pepper, to taste

Directions:

1. In the soup maker, add all ingredients. Be careful not to overfill your soup maker.
2. Close the lid and cook on smooth setting.

Nutritional Value: Calories 146; Fat 8g; Carbohydrates 21g; Protein 2g

Recipe 36: Cheeky Chicken Soup

Serving Size: 2

Cooking Time: 35 minutes

Ingredients:

- 1 chopped onion
- 1 chopped large carrot
- 700ml / 23.7oz of chicken stock
- 150g / 5.3oz of skinless, shredded roast chicken
- 100g / 3.5oz frozen peas
- 1 ½ tablespoons of Greek yoghurt
- ½ small, crushed garlic clove
- Squeeze of lemon juice

Directions:

1. Add the carrots, onion, and peas to your soup maker
2. Choose the chunky soup program
3. Once the program ends stir in the chicken and leave to warm
4. Mix the garlic, yoghurt, and lemon juice together
5. Season and pour into bowls, add the rest of the yoghurt, and serve.

Nutritional Value: Calories 155; Fat 5g; Carbohydrates 8g; Protein 17g

Recipe 37: Cheesy Cauliflower Soup

Serving Size: 4

Cooking Time: 30 minutes

Ingredients:

- 250g / 1/3 of a cup of cauliflower florets
- 100g / 3.5oz of cheddar cheese
- 1 teaspoon of basil
- 300ml / 10.1oz water
- 200ml / 6.8oz milk
- 100ml / 3.4oz Greek yoghurt
- Salt and pepper

Directions:

1. Cut the prepared cauliflower into small florets and place in the bottom of your soup maker
2. Add the water and seasoning
3. Cook using the chunky soup for 28 minutes
4. Add the milk and Greek yoghurt and blend
5. Add the cheese and mix thoroughly
6. Serve and enjoy.

Nutritional Value: Calories 197; Fat 10g; Carbohydrates 13g; Protein 13g

Recipe 38: Chicken and Anellini Pasta Soup

Serving Size: 4

Cooking Time: 30 minutes

Ingredients:

- 1 tablespoon olive oil
- 200g/7oz skinless chicken breast, chopped
- 1 onion, chopped
- 125g/4oz anellini pasta
- 2 carrots, chopped
- 125g/4oz cauliflower florets
- 750ml/3 cups chicken stock
- 2 teaspoon dried herbs
- Salt & pepper to taste

Directions:

1. Add all the prepared ingredients to the soup maker. Cover and leave to actually cook on high for 30 minutes. Ensure all the ingredients are well combined, tender and piping hot.
2. Blend to your preferred consistency (or leave your machine to do this as programmed). Adjust the seasoning and serve.

Nutritional Value: Calories 176; Fat 11g; Carbohydrates 20g; Protein 6g

Recipe 39: Chicken Corn Soup

Serving Size: 4

Cooking Time: 30 minutes

Ingredients:

- 120g drained sweet corn
- 300g chicken breast, cooked, boneless, skinless, cut into shreds
- 2 carrots, peeled, diced
- 1 onion, peeled, diced
- 1 tablespoon parsley, chopped
- 2 tablespoons thyme, chopped
- 600ml hot chicken stock
- Salt, to taste
- Fresh ground black pepper, to taste

Directions:

1. In the soup maker, add onions, carrots, parsley, thyme, chicken, chicken stock, salt and black pepper.
2. Close the lid and cook on smooth setting.

Nutritional Value: Calories 130; Fat 7g; Carbohydrates 13g; Protein 5g

Recipe 40: Chicken Noodle Soup

Serving Size: 4

Cooking Time: 30 minutes

Ingredients:

- 350g/12oz boneless chicken thighs, cooked and chopped
- 1 medium onion, peeled and chopped
- 1 large carrot, peeled and chopped
- 1 stalk celery, trimmed
- 2 medium leeks, chopped
- 125g/4oz rice noodles
- 1lt/4 cups chicken stock
- Handful of spring onions/scallions to garnish

Directions:

2. Add all the prepared ingredients, except the spring onions, to the soup maker. Cover and leave to cook on high for 30 minutes. Ensure all the ingredients are well combined, tender and piping hot.
3. Blend on the chunky setting (or leave your machine to do this as programmed). Adjust the seasoning, and serve with the spring onions over the top.

Nutritional Value: Calories 138; Fat 9g; Carbohydrates 14g; Protein 8.4g

Recipe 41: Chickpea, Coriander and Cumin Seed Soup

Serving Size: 4

Cooking Time: 30 minutes

Ingredients:

- 1 tablespoon olive oil
- 300g/11oz tinned chickpeas, drained
- 1 red chilli, deseeded and chopped
- 2 teaspoon each coriander/cilantro seeds, crushed with a pestle & mortar
- 2 teaspoon cumin seeds, crushed with a pestle & mortar
- 4 cloves garlic, crushed
- 1 teaspoon ground turmeric
- 750ml/3 cups vegetable stock
- Zest of 1 lemon
- 2 tablespoon lemon juice
- Salt & pepper to taste

Directions:

1. Add all the prepared ingredients to the soup maker, except the lemon juice. Cover and leave to actually cook on high for 30 minutes. Ensure all the ingredients are well combined, tender and piping hot.
2. Blend to your preferred consistency (or leave your machine to do this as programmed). Add the lemon juice, adjust the seasoning and serve.

Nutritional Value: Calories 130; Fat 7g; Carbohydrates 13g; Protein 5g

Recipe 42: Chunky Cod Soup

Serving Size: 4

Cooking Time: 30 minutes

Ingredients:

- 2 tablespoon olive oil
- 2 medium onions, peeled and chopped
- 2 stalks celery, chopped
- 1lt/4 cups fish stock/broth
- 2 medium carrots, peeled and chopped
- 2 large potatoes, peeled and chopped
- 150g/5oz green beans, chopped
- 2 medium courgettes/zucchini, chopped
- 1 yellow bell pepper, de-seeded and chopped
- 1 400g/14oz tin chopped tomatoes
- Salt and pepper
- 550g/1¼lb cod fillets, skinned, cooked and cut into strips
- Handful of flat leaf parsley, roughly chopped

Directions:

1. Add all the ingredients, except the parsley, to the soup maker. Cover and leave to actually cook on high for 30 minutes. Ensure all the ingredients are well combined, tender and piping hot.
2. Blend to your preferred consistency (or leave your machine to do this as programmed). Stir in the parsley, adjust the seasoning and serve.

Nutritional Value: Calories 199; Fat 13g; Carbohydrates 5g; Protein 16g

Recipe 43: Colorful Coriander and Carrot Soup

Serving Size: 2

Cooking Time: 30 minutes

Ingredients:

- 1 chopped small onion
- 1 small peeled and chopped potato
- 400g / 14.1oz peeled and chopped carrots
- 600ml / 20.2oz of chicken or vegetable stock
- ½ bunch of coriander

Directions:

1. Put all your ingredients except the coriander into the soup maker and select the smooth soup program
2. Once complete, season the soup and add the coriander
3. Blend again until completely combined
4. Serve and enjoy.

Nutritional Value: Calories 133; Fat 2g; Carbohydrates 14g; Protein 9g

Recipe 44: Creamy Leek and Stilton Soup

Serving Size: 4

Cooking Time: 30 minutes

Ingredients:

- 2 leeks, sliced
- 950 ml vegetable stock
- 4.93 g. garlic, minced
- 1 onion, chopped
- 340 g. potato, peeled and diced
- 14.2 g. butter
- 230 g. Stilton cheese
- Pepper
- Salt

Directions:

1. Melt butter in a prepared saucepan over medium heat. Add onion and sauté for 2 minutes.
2. Add garlic and leek and sauté for 2-3 minutes or until leek is softened. Transfer sautéed onion, garlic, and leek to the soup maker.
3. Add remaining ingredients and stir well. Seal soup maker with lid and cook on smooth mode. Season soup with salt and pepper. Serve and enjoy.

Nutritional Value: Calories 136; Fat 3.2g; Carbohydrates 24.9g; Protein 3.2g

Recipe 45: French Spring Onion Soup

Serving Size: 4

Cooking Time: 30 minutes

Ingredients:

- Large knob of unsalted butter
- 1 tablespoon olive oil
- 10 spring onions/scallions, chopped
- 1 medium onion, peeled and chopped
- 2 tablespoon sherry
- 750ml/3 cups vegetable stock/broth
- 1 tablespoon lemon juice
- Salt and pepper
- Gruyère cheese, grated, to garnish

Directions:

1. Add all the prepared ingredients to the soup maker except the cheese and remaining butter. Cover and leave to actually cook on high for 30 minutes. Ensure all the ingredients are well combined, tender and piping hot.
2. Blend to your preferred consistency (or leave your machine to do this as programmed). Stir in the rest of the butter. Adjust the prepared seasoning and serve garnished with the grated cheese.

Nutritional Value: Calories 260; Fat 21g; Carbohydrates 9g; Protein 12g

Recipe 46: Lentil, Leek, and Carrot Soup

Serving Size: 4

Cooking Time: 15 minutes

Ingredients:

- 750ml // 3 cups vegetable or pork stock
- 75g // 2.5oz red lentils
- 3 carrots, finely chopped
- 1 medium leek, sliced
- Small handful of parsley to serve

Directions:

1. Put all the prepared ingredients except the parsley in a soup maker and use the chunky soup function. The soup may look a little foamy to begin with, but this will disappear once the lentils start to cook.
2. At the end of the cycle, check the lentils are cooked and tender, and season to taste. Serve with a scattering of parsley.

Nutritional Value: Calories 103; Fat 1g; Carbohydrates 15g; Protein 6g

Recipe 47: Mexican Chili Soup

Serving Size: 8

Cooking Time: 40 minutes

Ingredients:

- 1 tablespoon olive oil
- 1 medium onion, peeled and chopped
- 1 red or green chilli, chopped
- 2 cloves garlic, peeled and crushed
- 250g/8oz cooked minced/ground beef
- 1 400g/14oz tin chopped tomatoes
- 1 400g/14oz tin red kidney beans, drained and rinsed
- 750ml/3 cups beef stock/broth
- 2 squares dark chocolate
- Salt and pepper
- 1 tablespoon chopped fresh coriander/cilantro
- Dash of Tabasco sauce
- Soured cream to garnish
- Cheddar cheese, grated, to garnish

Directions:

1. Add all the ingredients except the coriander, sour cream and Tabasco to the soup maker. Cover and leave to actually cook on high for 40 minutes. Ensure all the ingredients are well combined, tender and piping hot.
2. Blend to your preferred consistency (or leave your machine to do this as programmed). Stir in the coriander and Tabasco. Adjust the seasoning and serve, garnished with soured cream and grated cheese.

Nutritional Value: Calories 217; Fat 0g; Carbohydrates 41g; Protein 10g

Recipe 48: Minestrone Homemade Soup

Serving Size: 6

Cooking Time: 35 minutes

Ingredients:

- 6 carrots
- 1 onion
- ½ bag of spinach
- 1 tin of tomatoes
- 50g / 1.8oz of frozen peas
- 2 teaspoons of tomato puree
- 150ml / 5.1oz of water
- 1 teaspoon of rosemary
- Salt and pepper
- 3 medium mushrooms
- Handful of brussels sprouts
- 3 fresh tomatoes
- 1 tin of kidney beans
- 2 teaspoons garlic puree
- 100g / 3.5oz pasta ditalini
- 1 teaspoon of oregano
- Handful of bay leavesl

Directions:

1. Peel and dice the prepared onion and carrots, then dice the mushrooms and tomato and put in the soup maker
2. Add the spinach, Brussel sprouts, peas, pasta, kidney beans and seasoning
3. Pour the prepared water over the ingredients and cook for 20 minutes on the chunky soup setting
4. Serve and enjoy.

Nutritional Value: Calories 217; Fat 0g; Carbohydrates 41g; Protein 10g

Recipe 49: Moroccan Carrot Soup

Serving Size: 4

Cooking Time: 30 minutes

Ingredients:

- 12 baby carrots, peeled, diced
- 4 inch ginger piece, peeled, chopped
- 1 red pepper, diced
- 1 onion, peeled, diced
- 100ml boiling water
- 1 can coconut milk
- 2 tablespoons coriander
- 2 teaspoons garlic puree
- 1 teaspoon turmeric
- 1 teaspoon cinnamon
- Salt, to taste
- Fresh ground black pepper, to taste

Directions:

1. In the soup maker, add carrots, ginger, red pepper, onion, boiling water, coconut milk, coriander, garlic puree, cinnamon, turmeric, salt and pepper. Be sure not to overfill your soup maker.
2. Close the lid and cook on smooth setting.
3. Once the soup maker cycle is complete, adjust seasonings and serve.

Nutritional Value: Calories 160; Fat 11g; Carbohydrates 10.4g; Protein 7.6g

Recipe 50: Mushroom, Cream and Herb Soup

Serving Size: 4

Cooking Time: 40 minutes

Ingredients:

- 1 tablespoon olive oil
- 1 leek, chopped
- 750ml/3 cups vegetable stock
- 450g/1lb chestnut mushrooms, chopped
- 1 garlic clove, crushed
- 120ml/½ cup low fat cream
- ½ teaspoon dried thyme
- ¼ teaspoon ground nutmeg
- 1 tablespoon plain/all-purpose flour
- 2 tablespoon finely chopped chives, to serve

Directions:

1. Add all the prepared ingredients to the soup maker except the cream and chives. Cover and leave to actually cook on high for 30 minutes. Ensure all the ingredients are well combined, tender and piping hot.
2. Blend to your preferred consistency (or leave your machine to do this as programmed). Stir through the cream, adjust the seasoning and serve with the chopped chives sprinkled on top.

Nutritional Value: Calories 137; Fat 6g; Carbohydrates 18g; Protein 5g

Recipe 51: Mushroom Soup

Serving Size: 4

Cooking Time: 10 minutes

Ingredients:

- 90g // 3oz butter
- 2 medium onions, roughly chopped
- 1 garlic clove, crushed
- 500g // 17.5oz mushrooms, finely chopped
- 2 tablespoon plain flour
- 1 litre // 4 cups chicken stock
- 4 tablespoon cream
- Small handful of flat-leaf parsley to serve

Directions:

1. Heat the butter gently in a large saucepan, and cook the onions and garlic until soft, but not browned. This should take between about 8 and 10 minutes.
2. Add the mushrooms and cook on a high heat until softened, and sprinkle over the flour before stirring to combine.
3. Add the contents of the large-sized pan to your soup maker and top up with the chicken stock.
4. Set the soup maker on smooth.
5. Once the cycle has finished, stir through the cream, and scatter the parsley over to serve.

Nutritional Value: Calories 309; Fat 22g; Carbohydrates 14g; Protein 11g

Recipe 52: Prawn and Okra Soup

Serving Size: 4

Cooking Time: 40 minutes

Ingredients:

- 1 tablespoon olive oil
- 125g/4oz cooked peeled prawns
- 750ml/3 cups fish or vegetable stock
- 125g/4oz okra, trimmed and sliced
- 1 onion, chopped
- 1 bay leaf (remove before blending)
- ¼ teaspoon ground all spice
- 50g/2oz long grain rice
- 1 tablespoon white wine vinegar
- 1 garlic cloves, crushed
- 2 teaspoon anchovy paste
- 2 tablespoon tomato puree/paste
- 2 slices lean back bacon, chopped
- Salt & pepper to taste

Directions:

1. Add all the prepared ingredients to the soup maker. Cover and leave to actually cook on high for 30-40 minutes. Ensure all the ingredients are well combined, tender and piping hot. Remove the bay leaf.
2. Blend to your preferred consistency (or leave your machine to do this as programmed). Adjust the seasoning and serve.

Nutritional Value: Calories 175; Fat 9g; Carbohydrates 15g; Protein 9g

Recipe 53: Ramen Pork Soup

Serving Size: 4

Cooking Time: 20 minutes

Ingredients:

- 1 teaspoon vegetable oil
- 225g/8oz ramen noodles
- 250g/9oz pork tenderloin, chopped
- 750ml/3 cups chicken stock
- Large bunch spring onions/scallions, chopped
- 1 tablespoon freshly grated ginger
- 225g/8oz ready to use bamboo shoots
- 2 tablespoon soy sauce
- 1 tablespoon rice wine vinegar
- 1 teaspoon brown sugar
- 75g/3oz spinach, chopped
- Salt & pepper to taste

Directions:

1. Add all the prepared ingredients to the soup maker. Cover and leave to actually cook on high for 20 minutes.
2. Ensure all the ingredients are well combined, tender and piping hot. Adjust the seasoning and serve.

Nutritional Value: Calories 176; Fat 11g; Carbohydrates 20g; Protein 6g

Recipe 54: Roasted Tomato Soup

Serving Size: 4

Cooking Time: 40 minutes

Ingredients:

- 8 ripe tomatoes, halved
- 750ml chicken stock
- 2 teaspoons tomato puree
- 1 teaspoon brown sugar
- 1 tablespoon olive oil
- 1 tablespoon balsamic vinegar
- 2 garlic cloves, chopped
- 2 red onions, chopped
- Salt, to taste
- Freshly ground black pepper, to taste

Directions:

1. Ready to cook? Heat your oven to 2000 C.
2. In a roasting tray, add onions, tomatoes, and garlic.
3. Mix together balsamic vinegar, olive oil, and salt and pepper in a bowl. Sprinkle the mixture over tomatoes.
4. Place in the prepared preheated oven to roast for 20 minutes.
5. Transfer tomatoes, garlic, and onions into the Soup Maker.
6. Add all ingredients. Close the lid and set on smooth.
7. Your soup will be ready in 20 to 25 minutes, depending on your Soup Maker timer.

Nutritional Value: Calories 138; Fat 9g; Carbohydrates 14g; Protein 8.4g

Recipe 55: Shallot Potato Soup

Serving Size: 4

Cooking Time: 27 minutes

Ingredients:

- 3 potatoes, peeled, diced
- 2 tablespoons olive oil
- ½ teaspoon cinnamon
- 1 teaspoon paprika
- 1 teaspoon salt
- 2 garlic cloves, minced
- 1 onion, chopped
- 1 vegetable stock cube
- 1 Liter boiling water
- Black pepper, to taste

Directions:

1. Set your pot on sauté function. Add olive oil. When hot, add prepared onions and cook for 3 to 5 minutes or until softened.
2. Add shallot and garlic. Cook for approximately about 1 to 2 minutes, stirring occasionally.
3. Add boiling water and stock cube. Stir to dissolve the stock cube.
4. Add all remaining ingredients. Close the lid and cook for 21 minutes on smooth.

Nutritional Value: Calories 181; Fat 13g; Carbohydrates 34g; Protein 16g

Recipe 56: Shiitake and Onion Noodle Soup

Serving Size: 4

Cooking Time: 20 minutes

Ingredients:

- 1 tablespoon olive oil
- 150g/5oz fine egg noodles
- 125g/4oz shiitake mushrooms, pre soaked and chopped
- 1 teaspoon each ground turmeric & garlic powder
- 1 teaspoon crushed chilli flakes
- 1 tablespoon freshly grated ginger
- 1 teaspoon brown sugar
- 750ml/3 cups chicken stock
- 2 teaspoon shrimp paste
- 1 regular white onion, chopped
- 1 red onion, cut into rings
- Salt & pepper to taste

Directions:

1. Add all the prepared ingredients to the soup maker, except the sliced red onion. Cover and leave to actually cook on high for 20 minutes.
2. Ensure all the ingredients are well combined, tender and piping hot. Adjust the seasoning and serve with the sliced red onions arranged on top of each bowl of soup.

Nutritional Value: Calories 199; Fat 13g; Carbohydrates 5g; Protein 16g

Recipe 57: Spiced Turkey and Chickpea Soup

Serving Size: 4

Cooking Time: 30 minutes

Ingredients:

- 1 tablespoon olive oil
- 250g/9oz lean turkey meat, chopped
- 1 onion, chopped
- 1 orange (bell) pepper, deseeded and chopped
- 1 teaspoon each ground turmeric & coriander/cilantro
- ½ teaspoon crushed chilli flakes
- 1 tablespoon mild curry powder
- 75g/3oz basmati rice
- 750ml/3 cups chicken stock
- 200g/7oz tinned chickpeas, drained
- 1 tablespoon freshly chopped coriander/cilantro
- Salt & pepper to taste

Directions:

1. Add all the prepared ingredients to the soup maker, except the chopped coriander. Cover and leave to actually cook on high for 30 minutes. Ensure all the ingredients are well combined, tender and piping hot.
2. Blend to your preferred consistency (or leave your machine to do this as programmed). Adjust the seasoning, sprinkle with chopped coriander and serve.

Nutritional Value: Calories 137; Fat 6g; Carbohydrates 18g; Protein 5g

Recipe 58: Spicy Vegetable Soup

Serving Size: 4

Cooking Time: 45 minutes

Ingredients:

- 2 tablespoon olive oil
- 2 medium onions, peeled and chopped
- 2 medium sweet potatoes, peeled and chopped
- 2 medium carrots, peeled and chopped
- 2 medium parsnips, peeled and chopped
- 2 teaspoon medium curry powder
- 75g/3oz dried green lentils
- 750ml/3 cups vegetable stock/broth
- 250ml/1 cup milk
- Salt and pepper
- Greek yogurt to garnish

Directions:

1. Add all the prepared ingredients, except the milk, to the soup maker. Cover and leave to cook on high for 40 minutes. Ensure all the ingredients are well combined, tender and piping hot.
2. Blend to your preferred consistency (or leave your machine to do this as programmed). Stir in the milk and warm through for a further 5 minutes. Adjust the seasoning and serve with a spoonful of yogurt.

Nutritional Value: Calories 160; Fat 11g; Carbohydrates 10.4g; Protein 7.6g

Recipe 59: Tarragon Chicken Soup

Serving Size: 4

Cooking Time: 30 minutes

Ingredients:

- 2 tablespoons tarragon, fresh, chopped
- 150g chicken, cooked, cut into shreds
- 1 pint hot chicken stock
- 150ml double cream
- 1 tablespoon olive oil
- 1 onion, peeled, chopped
- 2 garlic cloves, minced

Directions:

1. Turn your Soup Maker on SAUTE and add olive oil. Cook onions until tender. If your Soup Maker doesn't have this function, sauté onions in a small skillet and pour into the Soup Maker.
2. Add all remaining prepared ingredients and close the lid.
3. Set on smooth function.
4. Your soup will ready in 20 to 30 minutes.

Nutritional Value: Calories 235; Fat 9g; Carbohydrates 12g; Protein 6g

Recipe 60: Tuna and Bean Soup

Serving Size: 4

Cooking Time: 20 minutes

Ingredients:

- 1 tablespoon olive oil
- 1 medium onion, peeled and chopped
- 3 cloves garlic, peeled and chopped
- 1lt/4 cups chicken stock/broth
- 1 400g/14oz tin cannellini beans, drained and rinsed
- 165g/5oz tinned tuna, drained
- 1 handful kale, chopped
- 1 tablespoon parmesan cheese, grated
- Salt and pepper to taste

Directions:

1. Add all the prepared ingredients except the cheese to the soup maker. Cover and leave to actually cook on high for 20 minutes. Ensure all the ingredients are well combined, tender and piping hot.
2. Blend to your preferred consistency (or leave your machine to do this as programmed). Stir in the Parmesan until it melts. Adjust the seasoning and serve.

Nutritional Value: Calories 260; Fat 21g; Carbohydrates 9g; Protein 12g

Chapter 4:   Dinner Recipes

Recipe 61: Asparagus and Aubergine Soup

Serving Size: 4

Cooking Time: 40 minutes

Ingredients:

- 1 tablespoon olive oil
- 1 large onion, peeled and chopped
- 300g/11oz asparagus tips, chopped
- ½ aubergine/eggplant, peeled and chopped
- 1 medium potato, peeled and chopped
- 750ml/3 cups vegetable stock/broth
- 1 teaspoon sundried tomato puree/paste
- Salt & pepper

Directions:

1. Add all the prepared ingredients to the soup maker. Cover and leave to cook on high for 40 minutes. Ensure all the ingredients are well combined, tender and piping hot.
2. Blend to your preferred consistency (or leave your machine to do this as programmed). Adjust the seasoning and serve.

Nutritional Value: Calories 199; Fat 13g; Carbohydrates 5g; Protein 16g

Recipe 62: Bacon and Chestnut Soup

Serving Size: 4

Cooking Time: 30 minutes

Ingredients:

- 1 tablespoon olive oil
- 1 medium onion, peeled and chopped
- 5 rashers streaky bacon, cooked and chopped
- 1 stalk celery, chopped
- 2 medium carrots, peeled and chopped
- 200g/7oz vacuum-packed chestnuts
- 1lt/4 cups chicken or vegetable stock/broth
- Salt and freshly ground black pepper
- Few sprigs of thyme, to garnish

Directions:

1. Add all the ingredients except the thyme sprigs to the soup maker. Cover and leave to actually cook on high for 30 minutes. Ensure all the ingredients are well combined, tender and piping hot.
2. Blend to your preferred consistency (or leave your machine to do this as programmed). Adjust the seasoning, garnish with the fresh sprigs of thyme and serve.

Nutritional Value: Calories 181; Fat 13g; Carbohydrates 34g; Protein 16g

Recipe 63: Broccoli and Onion Soup

Serving Size: 3

Cooking Time: 30 minutes

Ingredients:

- 300g broccoli florets
- 1 onion, chopped
- 1 tablespoon corn flour
- 2 tablespoons water
- 2 tablespoons double cream
- 300ml semi skimmed milk
- 500ml hot chicken stock
- ½ teaspoon sea salt
- 1 pinch black pepper

Directions:

1. In a bowl, stir corn flour and water and pour into the soup maker. Add chicken stock, milk, onion, broccoli, salt and pepper.
2. Close the lid and cook on smooth setting.
3. Stir in double cream and serve.

Nutritional Value: Calories 176; Fat 11g; Carbohydrates 20g; Protein 6g

Recipe 64: Carrot and Celery Soup

Serving Size: 4

Cooking Time: 30 minutes

Ingredients:

- 2 cups celery ribs, chopped
- 3 carrots, peeled, chopped
- 1 onion, peeled, chopped
- 1 teaspoon parsley, fresh, chopped
- ½ teaspoon tarragon, dried
- 1 tablespoon extra-virgin olive oil
- 700ml hot vegetable stock
- Salt, to taste
- Fresh ground pepper, to taste

Directions:

1. Turn your soup maker on sauté and add olive oil. Cook onions until tender.
2. Add celery and carrots. Cook for approximately about 2 minutes and add the rest of ingredients. Be sure not to overfill your soup maker
3. Close the lid and cook on smooth.

Nutritional Value: Calories 138; Fat 9g; Carbohydrates 14g; Protein 8.4g

Recipe 65: Carrot and Spinach Soup

Serving Size: 2

Cooking Time: 25 minutes

Ingredients:

- 2 carrots, peeled, diced
- 200g spinach, chopped
- 700ml boiling water
- 1 onion, chopped
- 3 garlic cloves, chopped
- Salt and pepper, to taste
- 3 chillies, dried
- 30g cheddar

Directions:

1. In the Soup Maker, add carrots, spinach, onion, garlic, chillies, cheddar, and water.
2. Close the lid and select blend setting. Let your soup cook.
3. It takes approximately about 20 to 25 minutes, depending on your Soup Maker's settings.
4. Serve immediately and enjoy.

Nutritional Value: Calories 146; Fat 8g; Carbohydrates 21g; Protein 2g

Recipe 66: Cheddar Broccoli Soup

Serving Size: 6

Cooking Time: 25 minutes

Ingredients:

- 1 head broccoli, stem removed
- 50g cheddar cheese
- 1 onion, chopped
- 1 large potato, peeled, diced
- 1.25 pints hot vegetable stock
- Salt, to taste
- Freshly ground black pepper, to taste
- 1 tablespoon garlic, minced

Directions:

1. Add all ingredients into your Soup Maker. Set on smooth or chunky.
2. Leave your machine to make the soup.
3. It takes 20 to 25 minutes depending on the brand of your Soup Maker.

Nutritional Value: Calories 137; Fat 6g; Carbohydrates 18g; Protein 5g

Recipe 67: Chicken and Cheese Soup

Serving Size: 4

Cooking Time: 30 minutes

Ingredients:

- 1 tablespoon olive oil
- 225g/8oz cooked chicken breasts, chopped
- 1 medium onion, peeled and chopped
- 3 garlic cloves crushed
- 1 medium green bell pepper, de-seeded and chopped
- 1 400g/14oz tin chopped tomatoes
- 750ml/3 cups chicken stock
- 1 tablespoon fresh basil, chopped
- 2 teaspoon fresh oregano, chopped
- Pinch of crushed chilli
- 125g/4oz small soup pasta
- 1 tablespoon Parmesan cheese, grated, plus extra for garnish

Directions:

1. Add all the prepared ingredients, except the cheese and basil to the soup maker. Cover and leave to actually cook on high for 30 minutes. Ensure all the ingredients are well combined, tender and piping hot.
2. Blend to your preferred consistency (or leave your machine to do this as programmed). Stir in the parmesan. Adjust the prepared seasoning and serve, garnished with fresh basil.

Nutritional Value: Calories 175; Fat 9g; Carbohydrates 15g; Protein 9g

Recipe 68: Chicken and Sweetcorn Soup

Serving Size: 5

Cooking Time: 30 minutes

Ingredients:

- 250g chicken, cooked, cut into shreds
- 320g sweetcorn
- 100g water chestnuts, sliced
- 200g noodles, cooked, warm
- 750ml chicken stock
- 10g coriander, chopped
- 1 red onion, chopped
- 4 spring onions, chopped
- 1 red chili, seeds removed, chopped
- 1 teaspoon ginger, fresh, grated

Directions:

1. In the Soup Maker, add onions, water chestnuts, sweetcorn kernels, red onions, chicken shreds, and chicken stock.
2. Mix together corn flour and 1 teaspoon of water to form a smooth paste, and stir into broth mixture.
3. Stir to actually mix well and put the lid on.
4. Press chunky function and let your Soup Maker work her magic.
5. Serve soup over noodles and top with spring onions, coriander, and chili.

Nutritional Value: Calories 217; Fat 0g; Carbohydrates 41g; Protein 10g

Recipe 69: Chicken Mushroom Soup

Serving Size: 4

Cooking Time: 25 minutes

Ingredients:

- 2 leftover chicken legs
- 3 mushrooms, chopped
- ½ teaspoon garlic puree
- 3 teaspoons corn flour mixed with water
- 1 teaspoon butter
- 1 teaspoon mixed herbs
- 1 onion, chopped
- 1 carrot, chopped
- 1 pint hot chicken stock

Directions:

1. In the Soup Maker, add all ingredients. Close the lid and set on chunky feature.

Nutritional Value: Calories 181; Fat 13g; Carbohydrates 34g; Protein 16g

Recipe 70: Chili Broccoli Soup

Serving Size: 4

Cooking Time: 30 minutes

Ingredients:

- 1 teaspoon chili powder
- 1.2 liters boiling water
- 4 chicken stock cubes
- 2 onions, chopped
- 1 medium potato, peeled, chopped
- 1 broccoli stalk, chopped
- 1 teaspoon parmesan cheese
- Basil leaves, for garnish

Directions:

1. In the soup maker, add boiling water, chicken stock cubes, potatoes, onions, broccoli, and chili. Be sure not to overfill your soup maker. Close the lid and cook on smooth setting.
2. Once the soup maker cycle is complete, stir in cheese.
3. Serve with fresh basil leaves
4. If desired, season with salt and pepper

Nutritional Value: Calories 160; Fat 11g; Carbohydrates 10.4g; Protein 7.6g

Recipe 71: Chili Carrot and Potato Soup

Serving Size: 4

Cooking Time: 30 minutes

Ingredients:

- 1 liter boiling water
- 1 teaspoon chili flakes
- 1 teaspoon paprika
- 1 vegetable stock cube
- 1 onion, peeled, chopped
- 1 carrot, peeled, chopped
- 3 small potatoes, peeled, diced

Directions:

1. In the soup maker, add carrot, onion, potatoes, boiling water, vegetable stock cubes, chili flakes, and paprika. Be sure not to overfill your soup maker.
2. Close the lid and cook on smooth setting.

Nutritional Value: Calories 215; Fat 6.6g; Carbohydrates 14g; Protein 26.6g

Recipe 72: Chili Cauliflower Soup

Serving Size: 4

Cooking Time: 30 minutes

Ingredients:

- 1 teaspoon sweet chili powder
- 350g cauliflower, cut into florets
- 25g parmesan cheese, grated
- 200ml cream
- 700ml hot vegetable stock
- 1 pinch nutmeg
- 1 tablespoon tarragon

Directions:

2. In the soup maker, add cauliflower, parmesan, chili, nutmeg, tarragon, cream, and vegetable stock. Be sure not to overfill your soup maker.
3. Close the lid and cook on smooth function.

Nutritional Value: Calories 235; Fat 9g; Carbohydrates 12g; Protein 6g

Recipe 73: Creamy Broccoli and Cauliflower Soup

Serving Size: 6

Cooking Time: 30 minutes

Ingredients:

- 1 head cauliflower, cut into florets
- 1 head broccoli, cut into florets
- 1 medium potato, peeled, diced
- 1 carrot, peeled, diced
- 1 leek, diced
- 2 minced garlic clove
- ¼ teaspoon sea salt
- ¼ teaspoon fresh ground black pepper
- 2 tablespoons all-purpose flour
- 2 tablespoons butter, melted
- 200ml skimmed milk
- 600ml hot vegetable stock

Directions:

1. Turn your soup maker on sauté function and heat butter.
2. Once melted, cook leek and carrots for 4 minutes. Stir in garlic and cook for approximately about 1 minute. Add stock, skim milk, and flour. Stir to mix well. Add all remaining prepared ingredients and close the lid. Be sure not to overfill your soup maker.
3. Cook on smooth setting.

Nutritional Value: Calories 135; Fat 6.6g; Carbohydrates 34g; Protein 26.6g

Recipe 74: Curried Carrot Soup

Serving Size: 4

Cooking Time: 30 minutes

Ingredients:

- 700ml hot vegetable stock
- 2 carrots, peeled, chopped
- 1 onion, chopped
- 2 teaspoons curry powder
- 100ml crème fraiche
- Salt and pepper, to taste

Directions:

1. Add carrots, potatoes, onions, curry powder, vegetable stock, salt and pepper into the soup maker. Be sure not to overfill your soup maker.
2. Close the lid and cook on smooth setting.
3. Add crème fraiche, stir gently and serve.

Nutritional Value: Calories 175; Fat 9g; Carbohydrates 15g; Protein 9g

Recipe 75: Leek and Back Bacon Soup

Serving Size: 4

Cooking Time: 30 minutes

Ingredients:

- 1 tablespoon olive oil
- 200g/7oz lean back bacon, chopped
- 1 onion, chopped
- 2 leeks, chopped
- 200g/7oz potatoes, peeled & cubed
- 1 carrot, chopped
- 50g/2oz pearl barley
- 750ml/3 cups chicken stock
- Salt & pepper to taste

Directions:

1. Add all the prepared ingredients to the soup maker. Cover and leave to actually cook on high for 30 minutes. Ensure all the ingredients are well combined, tender and piping hot.
2. Blend to your preferred consistency (or leave your machine to do this as programmed). Adjust the seasoning and serve.

Nutritional Value: Calories 137; Fat 6g; Carbohydrates 18g; Protein 5g

Recipe 76: Leftover Meat Soup

Serving Size: 4

Cooking Time: 20 minutes

Ingredients:

- 1 tablespoon olive oil
- 1 medium onion, peeled and chopped
- 1 large carrot, peeled and chopped
- 1 stalk celery, chopped
- 1 clove garlic, crushed
- 1 400g/14oz tin tomatoes
- 1 400g/140z tin kidney beans, drained and rinsed
- 750ml/3 cups chicken stock/broth
- 200g/7oz cooked meat, chopped or shredded
- Salt and freshly ground black pepper
- Handful of parsley leaves, to garnish

Directions:

1. Add all the prepared ingredients, except the meat and parsley, to the soup maker. Cover and leave to actually cook on high for 20 minutes. Ensure all the ingredients are well combined, tender and piping hot.
2. Blend to your preferred consistency (or leave your machine to do this as programmed). Stir in the chopped meat and leave to heat through for another few minutes. Adjust the seasoning, and serve garnished with parsley.

Nutritional Value: Calories 135; Fat 6.6g; Carbohydrates 34g; Protein 26.6g

Recipe 77: Pea and Lettuce Soup

Serving Size: 4

Cooking Time: 35 minutes

Ingredients:

- Knob of butter
- 2 medium leeks, sliced
- 750ml/3 cups vegetable stock/broth
- 2 medium potatoes, peeled and chopped
- 200g/7oz sugar snap peas, trimmed
- 2 romaine hearts, chopped
- 3 tablespoon fresh tarragon
- 250ml/1 cup single cream
- Salt and pepper to taste

Directions:

1. Add all the ingredients, except the chopped romaine, tarragon and cream, to the soup maker. Cover and leave to actually cook on high for 30 minutes. Add the chopped romaine and tarragon, stir and leave to cook for a further 5 minutes. Ensure all the ingredients are well combined, tender and piping hot.
2. Blend to your preferred consistency (or leave your machine to do this as programmed). Stir in the cream. Adjust the seasoning and serve.

Nutritional Value: Calories 199; Fat 13g; Carbohydrates 5g; Protein 16g

Recipe 78: Pea Minty Soup

Serving Size: 4

Cooking Time: 28 minutes

Ingredients:

- 500g / 17.6oz of frozen garden peas
- 2 tablespoons / 1/8 of a cup of Greek yoghurt
- 2 peeled onions
- 1 teaspoon of fresh mint
- 50g / 1/3 of a cup of mozzarella cheese
- 250ml / 8.5oz water
- 1 teaspoon garlic puree
- 1 tablespoon of parsley
- Salt and pepper

Directions:

1. Dice the onion and then add all ingredients to soup maker
2. Cook for 25 minutes using the blend function
3. Add further water or yoghurt if required
4. Serve and enjoy.

Nutritional Value: Calories 168; Fat 3g; Carbohydrates 24g; Protein 11g

Recipe 79: Pork Hot and Sour Soup

Serving Size: 4

Cooking Time: 30 minutes

Ingredients:

- 1 tablespoon olive oil
- 1 handful shitake mushrooms pre-soaked & chopped
- 200g/7oz pork tenderloin, chopped
- 75g/3oz ready to use bamboo shoots
- 125g/4oz tofu, cubed
- 1 tablespoon tamarind paste
- 750ml/3 cups chicken stock
- 3 tablespoon rice wine vinegar
- 1 tablespoon soy sauce
- ½ teaspoon crushed chilli flakes
- Bunch spring onions/scallions, chopped
- Salt & pepper to taste

Directions:

1. Add all the prepared ingredients to the soup maker. Cover and leave to actually cook on high for 30 minutes. Ensure all the ingredients are well combined, tender and piping hot.
2. Blend to your preferred consistency (or leave your machine to do this as programmed). Adjust the seasoning and serve.

Nutritional Value: Calories 176; Fat 11g; Carbohydrates 20g; Protein 6g

Recipe 80: Pumpkin Soup

Serving Size: 2

Cooking Time: 30 minutes

Ingredients:

- 500g pumpkin, peeled, diced
- 2 teaspoons mixed herbs
- 1 onion, peeled, chopped
- 3 garlic cloves, peeled, chopped
- Salt, to taste
- Fresh ground black pepper, to taste
- 400ml hot vegetable stock

Directions:

1. Add vegetable stock, onions, pumpkin, garlic, salt, and pepper into the soup maker.
2. Close the lid and cook on smooth setting.

Nutritional Value: Calories 138; Fat 9g; Carbohydrates 14g; Protein 8.4g

Recipe 81: Roast Chicken Soup

Serving Size: 2

Cooking Time: 15 minutes

Ingredients:

- 1 onion, chopped
- 1 large carrot, chopped
- 1 teaspoon thyme leaves, roughly chopped
- 700ml // 3 cups chicken stock
- 100g // 3.5oz frozen peas
- 150g // 5oz leftover roast chicken, shredded
- 1.5 tablespoon Greek yogurt
- Small garlic clove, crushed
- Squeeze of lemon juice

Directions:

1. Put the onion, carrots, thyme, stock, and peas in the soup maker, and use the chunky soup function.
2. Once the cycle is complete, stir the shredded roast chicken, and use the soup maker's warm function to heat the chicken.
3. Mix the prepared yogurt, garlic, and lemon juice together.
4. Season the soup and pour into bowls. Serve with a swirl of the yogurt mixture.

Nutritional Value: Calories 155; Fat 5g; Carbohydrates 8g; Protein 17g

Recipe 82: Roast Dinner Soup

Serving Size: 4

Cooking Time: 13 minutes

Ingredients:

- 30g / 1.1oz turkey
- 100g / 3.5oz instant cauliflower cheese
- 5 parsnips, roasted
- 25g / 0.9oz brussels sprouts
- 1 teaspoon chives
- Salt and pepper
- 2 yorkshire puddings
- 5 roast potatoes
- 2 tablespoons of mash potato
- 1 tablespoon of gravy
- 2 teaspoons of parsley
- 150ml / 5fl oz of water

Directions:

1. Chop all ingredients and put them in the soup maker
2. Add the water
3. Add the seasoning and set the soup maker to the blend function then cook for 10 minutes
4. As the ingredients are already cooked you are just blending and heating them up
5. Serve and enjoy.

Nutritional Value: Calories 288; Fat 9g; Carbohydrates 42g; Protein 10g

Recipe 83: Roasted Cauliflower and Turmeric Soup

Serving Size: 6

Cooking Time: 30 minutes

Ingredients:

- 1 medium cauliflower head, cut into florets, roasted
- 2.46 g. dried parsley
- ½ carrot, peeled and chopped
- 9.86 g. turmeric powder
- ½ celery, peeled and chopped
- 2.46 g. dried mix herbs
- 240 ml of water
- 66 ml yogurt
- 1 bell pepper
- 1 small butternut squash, peeled and chopped
- 1 onion, chopped
- Pepper
- Salt

Directions:

1. Add all ingredients except yogurt into the soup maker. Seal soup maker with lid and cook for 25 minutes on blend mode.
2. Add yogurt and stir well. Season soup with salt and pepper. Serve and enjoy.

Nutritional Value: Calories 76; Fat 2g; Carbohydrates 12g; Protein 4g

Recipe 84: Smoked Haddock Chowder with Sweet Corn

Serving Size: 4

Cooking Time: 32 minutes

Ingredients:

- 340 g. haddock, smoked fillets, undyed, diced
- 591 ml. milk
- 2 leeks, cleaned and trimmed, diced
- 1 bay leaf
- ½ carrot, peeled and diced
- 1 onion, diced
- 16 g. flour, all-purpose
- 2 medium potatoes, peeled, cooked mashed
- 56 g. butter
- 30 g. baby spinach, leaves only, shredded
- 177 ml heavy cream (or double cream)
- 123 g. sweet corn, canned
- Pepper
- Salt
- 14 g. Parsley (flat leaf)

Directions:

1. Transfer all your ingredients, except the bay leaf and sweet corn to the soup maker and stir well.
2. Seal soup maker with lid and cook on smooth mode.
3. When done, switch off the Soup Maker, stir in bay leaf and sweet corn.
4. Cover and allow to sit so the bay leaf can be infused for about 5 minutes.
5. Discard bay leaf. Season soup with salt and pepper. Serve and enjoy.

Nutritional Value: Calories 313; Fat 10g; Carbohydrates 30g; Protein 26g

Recipe 85: Spicy Carrot and Ginger Soup

Serving Size: 4

Cooking Time: 40 minutes

Ingredients:

- 680 g carrots, peeled and chopped
- 2 cloves garlic, crushed
- 8.4 g ginger, ground
- 15 ml olive oil
- 950 ml chicken broth
- 15 ml lemon juice
- 1 onion, chopped
- Pepper
- Salt

Directions:

1. Heat oil in a prepared pan over medium heat. Add the prepared onion and garlic and sauté until onion is softened. Transfer to the soup maker.
2. Add remaining ingredients to the soup maker and stir well. Seal soup maker with lid and cook on smooth mode for 21 minutes.
3. Season soup with salt and pepper. Serve and enjoy.

Nutritional Value: Calories 226; Fat 8g; Carbohydrates 34g; Protein 9g

Recipe 86: Tomato and Red Pepper Soup

Serving Size: 4

Cooking Time: 30 minutes

Ingredients:

- Knob of butter
- 1 medium onion, peeled and chopped
- 1 clove garlic, crushed
- 2 medium red bell peppers, de-seeded and chopped
- 1½ tablespoon tomato puree/paste
- 1 teaspoon smoked paprika
- 1 400g/14oz tin peeled plum tomatoes with basil
- 750ml/3 cups vegetable stock/broth
- ½ teaspoon brown sugar
- Salt and pepper to taste
- 60ml/¼ cup double cream
- 1 tablespoon chopped fresh basil

Directions:

1. Add all the ingredients, except the basil and cream, to the soup maker. Cover and leave to actually cook on high for 30 minutes. Ensure all the ingredients are well combined, tender and piping hot.
2. Blend to your preferred consistency (or leave your machine to do this as programmed). Stir in the basil and cream. Adjust the seasoning and serve.

Nutritional Value: Calories 260; Fat 21g; Carbohydrates 9g; Protein 12g

Recipe 87: Tomato Butternut Squash

Serving Size: 4

Cooking Time: 25 minutes

Ingredients:

- 1 tin tomatoes, chopped
- 250g tomato passata
- 400g butternut squash, cubed, roasted
- 1 teaspoon balsamic vinegar
- 3 teaspoons sugar
- 2 teaspoons garlic clove, minced
- 1 carrot, peeled, diced
- 1 white onion, chopped
- 1 chilli, chopped
- 1 red onion, chopped
- 1.5 pint chicken stock

Directions:

1. In the Soup Maker, add all ingredients and close the lid.
2. Set on smooth and creamy feature.
3. When ready, taste and season with salt and pepper if desired.
4. Serve and enjoy.

Nutritional Value: Calories 137; Fat 6g; Carbohydrates 18g; Protein 5g

Recipe 88: Tomato Chili Bean Soup

Serving Size: 4

Cooking Time: 25 minutes

Ingredients:

- 400g tin kidney beans
- 400g tin tomatoes, chopped
- 1 teaspoon chili pepper
- ½ teaspoon cumin powder
- 1 tablespoon olive oil
- 1 tablespoon tomato puree
- 1 garlic clove, minced
- 1 red pepper, chopped
- 1 onion, chopped
- Salt, to taste
- Freshly ground black pepper, to taste
- 500ml vegetable stock

Directions:

1. Turn your Soup Maker on sauté and add oil. When hot, sauté onions for 3 minutes. Add cumin, chili powder, and garlic. Cook for 1 minute.
2. If your Soup Maker has no sauté function, you can do this in a skillet and transfer the mixture into the Soup Maker.
3. Add all remaining prepared ingredients and close the lid. Set on smooth or chunky.
4. When ready, taste and season with salt and pepper.

Nutritional Value: Calories 146; Fat 8g; Carbohydrates 21g; Protein 2g

Recipe 89: Turkey and Mushroom Soup

Serving Size: 4

Cooking Time: 20 minutes

Ingredients:

- 1 tablespoon olive oil
- 1 medium onion, peeled and chopped
- 1lt/4 cups chicken stock/broth
- 2 teaspoon chopped fresh mixed herbs, e.g. sage and thyme
- Salt and freshly ground black pepper
- 250g/8oz mushrooms, sliced
- 120ml/½ cup milk
- 125g/4oz cooked turkey meat, finely chopped or shredded

Directions:

1. Add all the prepared ingredients, except the turkey to the soup maker. Cover and leave to actually cook on high for 20 minutes. Ensure all the ingredients are well combined, tender and piping hot.
2. Blend to your preferred consistency (or leave your machine to do this as programmed). Stir in the turkey pieces and leave to warm through for a few minutes. Adjust the seasoning, and serve.

Nutritional Value: Calories 160; Fat 11g; Carbohydrates 10.4g; Protein 7.6g

Recipe 90: Winter Vegetable Soup

Serving Size: 4

Cooking Time: 30 minutes

Ingredients:

- 150g leek, chopped
- 100g carrot, chopped
- 200g baby potatoes, whole, peeled
- 150g red onion, chopped
- 50g butter
- 800ml hot vegetable stock

Directions:

1. Turn your machine on sauté mode. Once hot, add butter and wait for it to melt.
2. Cook onions and leek for 4 minutes or until tender.
3. Add carrot, potato and vegetable stock.
4. Put the cover lid on and select smooth soup setting.
5. Once the cycle is complete, season as desired and serve.

Nutritional Value: Calories 175; Fat 9g; Carbohydrates 15g; Protein 9g

Chapter 5:   Dessert Recipes

Recipe 91: Apple and Parsnip Soup

Serving Size: 4

Cooking Time: 15 minutes

Ingredients:

- 1 tablespoon olive oil
- 2 Granny Smith apples
- 4 parsnips
- 1 teaspoon ground cinnamon
- 1 onion
- 1 litre // 4 cups vegetable stock

Directions:

1. Peel and chop the prepared apples, parsnips, and onion.
2. Heat the oil in a large-sized pan and sauté the onion.
3. Add the ingredients to the soup maker. You may need to top up with a little hot water if the actual stock does not reach the MIN level. Alternatively, if you would like a thicker soup, add more parsnips and apples.

Nutritional Value: Calories 210; Fat 5.6g; Carbohydrates 9.1g; Protein 2.5g

Recipe 92: Apple Pumpkin Soup

Serving Size: 4

Cooking Time: 30 minutes

Ingredients:

- 120 g green apple, chopped
- 238 g pumpkin, cubed
- 1 onion, chopped
- 3.28 garlic, chopped
- 30 ml olive oil
- 475 g vegetable stock
- Pepper
- Salt

Directions:

1. Heat oil in a prepared medium-sized pan over medium heat. Add onion and garlic and sauté for 2-3 minutes. Transfer to the soup maker.
2. Add remaining ingredients to the soup maker and stir well. Seal soup maker with lid and cook on smooth mode for 20 minutes.
3. Season soup with salt and pepper. Serve and enjoy.

Nutritional Value: Calories 146; Fat 8g; Carbohydrates 21g; Protein 2g

Recipe 93: Caramelized French Onion Soup

Serving Size: 4

Cooking Time: 30 minutes

Ingredients:

- 1 tablespoon olive oil
- 500g/1lb 2oz onions, sliced
- 3 cloves garlic, crushed
- 1 teaspoon brown sugar
- 250ml/1 cup dry white wine
- 500ml/2 cups vegetable stock
- Salt & pepper to taste

Directions:

1. Add all the prepared ingredients to the soup maker. Cover and leave to eventually cook on high for 30 minutes.
2. Ensure all the ingredients are well combined, tender and piping hot.
3. Blend to your preferred consistency (or leave your machine to do this as programmed). Adjust the seasoning and serve.

Nutritional Value: Calories 160; Fat 11g; Carbohydrates 10.4g; Protein 7.6g

Recipe 94: Carrot and Orange Soup

Serving Size: 4

Cooking Time: 10 minutes

Ingredients:

- 600g carrots, peeled and chopped
- 1 onion, chopped
- 600ml vegetable stock
- 300ml fresh orange juice
- 3tablespoon crème fraiche

Directions:

1. Add all prepared ingredients except the orange juice and crème fraiche to your soup maker and stir to combine well.
2. Ensure you don't actually go above the MAX line in your soup maker. If needed, top up to the MIN line with hot water.
3. Put the cover lid on and select the smooth setting.
4. Remove the lid and stir in the orange juice and crème fraiche. Manually blend for 10 to 20 seconds.

Nutritional Value: Calories 138; Fat 9g; Carbohydrates 14g; Protein 8.4g

Recipe 95: Chicken and Sweetcorn Soup

Serving Size: 5

Cooking Time: 30 minutes

Ingredients:

- 250g chicken, cooked, cut into shreds
- 320g sweetcorn
- 100g water chestnuts, sliced
- 200g noodles, cooked, warm
- 750ml chicken stock
- 10g coriander, chopped
- 1 red onion, chopped
- 4 spring onions, chopped
- 1 red chili, seeds removed, chopped
- 1 teaspoon ginger, fresh, grated

Directions:

1. In the Soup Maker, add onions, water chestnuts, sweetcorn kernels, red onions, chicken shreds, and chicken stock.
2. Mix together corn flour and 1 teaspoon of water to form a smooth paste, and stir into broth mixture.
3. Stir to actually mix well and put the lid on.
4. Press chunky function and let your Soup Maker work her magic.
5. Serve soup over noodles and top with spring onions, coriander, and chili.
6. Note: Be sure not to overfill your machine.

Nutritional Value: Calories 176; Fat 11g; Carbohydrates 20g; Protein 6g

Recipe 96: Sweet Potato and Coconut Milk Soup

Serving Size: 4

Cooking Time: 30 minutes

Ingredients:

- 1 tablespoon olive oil
- 2 onions, chopped
- 3 garlic cloves, crushed
- 1 tablespoon freshly grated ginger
- ½ teaspoon crushed chilli flakes (more or less to taste)
- 1 tablespoon medium curry powder
- 500g/1lb 2oz sweet potatoes, peeled & cubed
- 500ml/2 cups vegetable stock
- 250ml/1 cup low fat coconut milk
- 1 tablespoon lime juice
- 1 tablespoon freshly chopped coriander/cilantro
- Salt & pepper to taste

Directions:

1. Add all the prepared ingredients, except the coconut milk to the soup maker. Cover and leave to cook on high for 30 minutes.
2. Ensure all the ingredients are well combined, tender and piping hot. Blend to your preferred consistency (or leave your machine to do this as programmed).
3. Stir through the coconut milk and leave to gently warm through. Adjust the seasoning and serve.

Nutritional Value: Calories 235; Fat 9g; Carbohydrates 12g; Protein 6g

Recipe 97: Sweet Potato and Coconut Soup

Serving Size: 1

Cooking Time: 15 minutes

Ingredients:

- 1 tablespoon olive oil
- 1 medium onion, sliced
- 2 cloves garlic, crushed
- 300g sweet potato, peeled and chopped
- 250ml reduced fat coconut milk
- 2 teaspoon ground coriander
- 700ml vegetable stock

Directions:

1. Heat the oil in your soup maker if it has a sauté function. Alternatively heat the oil in a saucepan.
2. Add the chopped onions and sauté for 5 minutes. Add the garlic, sweet potato and coriander and sauté for a further 2 to 3 minutes, stirring frequently.
3. Switch off the sauté function on your soup maker/transfer ingredients to your soup maker.
4. Add the remaining ingredients. Ensure you are actually between the MIN and MAX lines on your soup maker. Add more hot water if required.
5. Set on smooth function.

Nutritional Value: Calories 176; Fat 11g; Carbohydrates 20g; Protein 6g

Recipe 98: Sweet Potato and Leek Soup

Serving Size: 4

Cooking Time: 15 minutes

Ingredients:

- 1 tablespoon olive oil
- 1 medium onion, chopped
- 2 garlic cloves, crushed
- 3 medium leeks (approx. 300g), chopped
- 2 sweet potatoes (approx. 300g), peeled and chopped
- 800ml vegetable stock
- 1 tablespoon fresh parsley, chopped (optional for garnish)

Directions:

1. Heat the olive oil in your soup maker if it has a sauté function, if not, heat it in a saucepan.
2. Add the prepared onion and garlic and sauté for about 3-5 minutes.
3. Switch off the sauté function on your soup maker/transfer from saucepan to soup maker.
4. Add remaining ingredients, apart from the parsley. Stir to combine well.
5. Ensure you don't actually go above the MAX line in your soup maker. If needed, top up to the MIN line with hot water.
6. Put the cover lid on and select the smooth setting.
7. Garnish with chopped parsley (optional).

Nutritional Value: Calories 164; Fat 9g; Carbohydrates 10.2g; Protein 8g

Recipe 99: Sweet Squash and Sunflower Seed Soup

Serving Size: 4

Cooking Time: 40 minutes

Ingredients:

- 1 tablespoon olive oil
- 1 tablespoon sunflower seeds, chopped
- 450g/1lb butternut squash flesh, peeled and cubed
- 200g/7oz potatoes, peeled and cubed
- 750ml/3 cups vegetable stock
- 60ml/ ½ cup low fat cream
- Salt & pepper to taste

Directions:

1. Add all the prepared ingredients to the soup maker, except the sunflower seeds and cream. Cover and leave to actually cook on high for 40 minutes.
2. Ensure all the ingredients are well combined, tender and piping hot. Blend to your preferred consistency (or leave your machine to do this as programmed).
3. Stir through the cream and leave to warm for a minute or two. Adjust the seasoning and serve with the sunflower seeds sprinkled on top.

Nutritional Value: Calories 260; Fat 21g; Carbohydrates 9g; Protein 12g

Recipe 100:   Sweetcorn Soup

Serving Size: 4

Cooking Time: 15 minutes

Ingredients:

- 500g sweetcorn, drained
- 630ml vegetable stock
- 70ml cream
- Salt and black pepper, to taste

Directions:

1. In a soup maker, add sweetcorn, vegetable stock, and cream.
2. Season with salt and pepper.
3. Put on cream setting.

Nutritional Value: Calories 137; Fat 6g; Carbohydrates 18g; Protein 5g

4.   Conclusion

How useful do you think the Soup Maker sounds after browsing these recipes?

Now that you've read some really tasty recipes, you probably are ready to try some for yourself. Soup Makers are becoming more and more common in kitchens around the world, and people are finding totally new ways of using them. Most of all though, when you try these recipes, you'll find out that you can make soup just like they do at your favorite comfort-food restaurant, in 20 minutes or so.

You'll be happy to serve more healthy vegetables to your family, since soup recipes are simply full of vegetable-centered dishes. As cooks and chefs have requested more features, the Soup Maker of today will also make smoothies, desserts and even salads for your family!

Cooking with the Soup Maker is simplicity itself. Toss in your ingredients, pour in your water or stock and push the button for the type of soup or other dish you want it to make for you. You can even add things to it if you decide you want extra ingredients.

You'll have no pans sitting in your sink when you let the Soup Maker cook for you. It lets you use the freshest ingredients to make the best in quality soups, and it's easy! You'll never buy restaurant soup again. We hope you will actually enjoy trying out the recipes we have shared with you in this e-book!

5. Index

Printed in Great Britain
by Amazon

12663307R00066

Fresh & Tasty

Muffins
and slices

R&R PUBLICATIONS MARKETING PTY LTD

Published by:
R&R Publications Marketing Pty Ltd
ABN 78 348 105 138
PO Box 254, Carlton North, Victoria 3054 Australia
Phone (61 3) 9381 2199 Fax (61 3) 9381 2689
E-mail: info@randrpublications.com.au
Website: www.randrpublications.com.au
Australia-wide toll-free: 1800 063 296

Fresh & Tasty Muffins and slices

Publisher: Richard Carroll
Creative Director: Aisling Gallagher
Cover Designer: Lucy Adams
Production Manager: Anthony Carroll
Food Photography: Robert Monro, Warren Webb, Andrew Warn, William
Meppem, Andrew Elton, Quentin Bacon, Gary Smith, Per Ericson
Food Stylists: Ann Fayle, Susan Bell, Coty Hahn, Janet Lodge, Di Kirby
Recipe Development: Ellen Argyriou, Di Kirby, Janet Lodge.
Proofreader: Paul Hassing

Disclaimer: The nutritional information listed with each recipe does not include the nutrient
content of garnishes or any accompaniments not listed in specific quantities in the ingredient
list. The nutritional information for each recipe is an estimate only, and may vary depending
on the brand of ingredients used, and due to natural biological variations in the composition
of natural foods such as meat, fish, fruit and vegetables. The nutritional information was
calculated by using the computer program Foodworks dietary analysis software (version
3.01, Xyris Software Pty. Ltd. Queensland Australia), and is based on the Australian food
composition tables and food manufacturers' data. Where not specified, ingredients are
always analysed as average or medium, not small or large. The analysis shown is for 100g of
the recipe specified.

Includes Index
ISBN 1 74022 218 0
EAN 9 781740 222 18 1

First Printed April 2004
Reprinted January 2005 and August 2005
This Edition Printed January 2006
Computer Typeset in Futura

Printed in Singapore

Cover: Sticky Chocolate and Raspberry Sauce, Page 40

10

Contents

41

54

Introduction

Nothing beats the taste of home-baked cakes and biscuits. Yet today, many people think of these goodies as nothing more than a delightful memory.

This need not be so. This book will show that baking is not only an easy and affordable way to fill lunch boxes and provide snacks for your family, it's also fun.

Here you'll find a host of easy to make recipes that will bring those distant memories of freshly baked treats back to life. Baking has never been simpler or more fun than with this selection of quick and easy cakes and bakes. A bowl, a beater and a few minutes in the kitchen is all it takes to fill the house with the homey warmth and aroma that only a homemade muffin, cake or batch of biscuits can provide. There's a recipe in these pages to please everyone and every occasion. So, discover the pleasure of home baking and watch your friends and family return for more.

Baking secrets

When adding fresh fruit to batter it's best to follow the following advice: Whole berries and chopped fresh fruit are less likely to sink to the bottom of muffins and other quick breads during baking if you dredge them in flour first. Then shake off the excess flour in a colander before adding them to the batter. Besides helping to suspend the fruit evenly throughout the batter, the flour coating stops moist pieces of fruit from clumping together.

The basic ingredients in muffins – flour, flavourings, perhaps some leavening, and liquid – are the same ones used in almost a dozen other varieties of quick breads. Creating such amazing diversity from a few common staples is largely a matter of adjusting the proportions of dry and liquid ingredients. Use two parts dry to one part liquid ingredients and you get a thicker batter for baking muffins or loaves. Thicker still, with a ratio of dry to liquid ingredients approaching three to one, are soft doughs for cut biscuits and scones.

Muffins and most quick breads are best eaten soon after baking. Those that contain fruit, nuts, vegetables or moderately high amounts of fat stay moist longer than those low in fat. If muffins are left over, it's best to place them in the freezer in an airtight container, where they'll keep for up to 12 months.To reheat, bake the frozen muffins, wrapped in foil, at 175°C for 15–20 minutes, or until heated through. You can also store quick breads and biscuits in the same way.

An accurate oven is essential for successful baking. It should be well insulated and draught-proof, as a discrepancy of a few degrees can ruin baked goods. Regular checking with an oven thermometer helps avoid baking failures.

Muffins

The perfect muffin has a gently rounded top, a golden crust, a moist finely-grained crumb, an appealing aroma and a satisfying balance of flavour. Muffins are mini-cakes for busy home bakers. Freeze them for brunch treats, quick snacks and school lunch boxes, or when you need to stop and take a well-earned break.

Sweet Corn and Cheese Muffins

250g self-raising flour
1/2 tsp salt
315g can sweet corn kernels, drained
60g cheddar cheese, grated
2 tbsp grated Parmesan cheese
1 egg, lightly beaten
185mL milk
45g butter, melted

1 Sift flour and salt together in a bowl. Mix in sweet corn, cheddar cheese and Parmesan cheese. Make a well in the centre of the dry ingredients.

2 Place egg, milk and butter in a small bowl and whisk to combine. Pour milk mixture into dry ingredients and mix with a fork until ingredients are just combined.

3 Spoon mixture into 10 greased 250mL capacity muffin tins. Bake for 20–30 minutes or until muffins are cooked when tested with a skewer. Turn onto wire racks to cool.

Makes 10

Oven temperature 180°C, 350°F, Gas 4

Classic Blueberry Muffins

315g self-raising flour
1 tsp baking powder
90g sugar
2 eggs, lightly beaten
1 cup buttermilk or milk
60g butter, melted
125g blueberries
2 tbsp coffee sugar crystals*

1 Sift flour and baking powder together into a bowl, add sugar and mix to combine.

2 Combine eggs, milk and butter. Add egg mixture and blueberries to dry ingredients and mix until just combined.

3 Spoon mixture into 6 greased 250mL capacity muffin tins. Sprinkle with coffee sugar crystals and bake for 20–30 minutes or until muffins are cooked when tested with a skewer. Turn onto wire racks to cool.

Makes 6

Note: *Finely shredded orange rind can be added to this mixture to enhance the flavour of the blueberries.*

*Coffee sugar crystals are coarse golden brown sugar grains. If unavailable, raw (muscovado) or demerara sugar can be used instead.

Oven temperature 200°C, 400°F, Gas 6

Oatbran and Fruit Muffins

180g self-raising flour
30g oat bran
75g brown sugar
½ cup canola oil
2 eggs
125g dried fruit medley
1 cup buttermilk

1 Combine flour, oat, bran and brown sugar. Beat oil and eggs together and stir in the dry ingredients along with the fruit medley and buttermilk. Mix until just combined, do not over mix.

2 Spoon mixture onto lightly greased muffin pans. Bake in an oven at 190°C for 25–30 minutes.

Makes 12

Oven temperature 190°C, 370°F, Gas 5

Mini Sardine Muffins

180g self-raising flour
1 tbsp lemon thyme
pinch paprika
1 egg
60mL canola oil
180mL milk
125g can sardines in tomato
sauce, mashed

1   Combine flour, lemon thyme and paprika in a bowl. In a separate dish mix together the egg, oil and milk. Quickly and lightly combine the dry and liquid ingredients, then fold in the sardines.

2   Spoon mixture into lightly greased muffin pans or patty pans. Bake in an oven at 200°C for 12–14 minutes or until golden. Serve warm.

Makes 24

Oven temperature 200°C, 400°F, Gas 6

Tuna Puffs

2 eggs
60mL cream
1 bunch dill
black pepper to taste
30g Edam cheese, grated
185g can tuna, drained
and flaked

1 Beat together the eggs and cream, season to taste with dill and black pepper. Fold in the cheese and tuna.

2 Place spoonfuls of the mixture into lightly greased muffin pans or patty pans.

3 Bake in an oven at 200°C for 10–12 minutes or until puffed and golden. Serve hot or warm.

Makes 12

Oven temperature 200°C, 400°F, Gas 6

Apricot Oatbran Muffins

250g self-raising flour
1 tsp baking powder
45g oat bran
60g dried apricots, chopped
60g sultanas
1 egg, lightly beaten
325mL buttermilk or milk
60mL golden syrup
90g butter, melted

1 Sift flour and baking powder together into a bowl. Add oat bran, apricots and sultanas, mix to combine and set aside.
2 Combine egg, milk, golden syrup and butter.
3 Add milk mixture to dry ingredients and mix until just combined. Spoon mixture into 6 greased 250mL capacity muffin tins and bake for 15–20 minutes or until muffins are cooked when tested with a skewer. Serve hot, warm or cold.

Makes 6

Note: Serve this muffin for breakfast or brunch fresh and warm from the oven, split and buttered and perhaps with a drizzle of honey.

Oven temperature 180°C, 350°F, Gas 4

Cornbread Muffins

185g self-raising flour
170g cornmeal (polenta)
45g grated Parmesan cheese
1 tsp baking powder
1 tsp ground cumin
pinch chilli powder
2 cups buttermilk or low-fat milk
2 eggs, lightly beaten
1 tbsp polyunsaturated vegetable oil

1 Place flour, cornmeal (polenta), Parmesan cheese, baking powder, cumin and chilli powder in a bowl and mix to combine.

2 Make a well in the centre of the flour mixture, add milk, eggs and oil and mix until just combined.

3 Spoon mixture into 12 greased 90mL muffin tins and bake for 30 minutes or until muffins are cooked when tested with a skewer.

Makes 12

*Note: Cornmeal (polenta) is cooked yellow maize flour and is very popular in northern Italian and southern American cooking.
It adds an interesting texture and flavour to baked products such as these muffins and is available from health-food stores and some supermarkets.*

Oven temperature 190°C, 375°F, Gas 5

Choc-Rough Muffins Photograph opposite

125g butter, softened
125g sugar
2 eggs, lightly beaten
250g self-raising flour, sifted
30g cocoa powder, sifted
155g chocolate chips
45g shredded coconut
185mL buttermilk or milk

1 Place butter and sugar in a bowl and beat until light and fluffy. Gradually beat in eggs.

2 Combine flour and cocoa powder. Add the flour mixture, chocolate chips, coconut and milk to the butter mixture and mix until just combined.

3 Spoon mixture into 6 greased 250mL capacity muffin tins and bake for 35 minutes or until muffins are cooked when tested with a skewer.

Makes 6

Note: Muffin tins without a non-stick finish should be greased (and, if desired, lined with paper baking cups) before use. Non-stick tins do not need lining but may need greasing; follow the manufacturer's instructions.

Oven temperature 180°C, 350°F, Gas 4

Cheesy Apple Muffins

165g wholemeal self-raising flour
1/4 tsp ground cinnamon
1/4 tsp ground nutmeg
1/4 tsp ground ginger
1/4 tsp ground cloves
1 tsp baking powder
45g oatbran
3 tbsp brown sugar
1 green apple, peeled and grated
125g ricotta cheese
2 tbsp polyunsaturated oil
180mL apple juice

1 Sift flour, cinnamon, nutmeg, ginger, cloves and baking powder into a mixing bowl. Add oatbran and sugar.

2 Make a well in the centre of the flour mixture. Stir in the apple, ricotta, oil and apple juice. Mix until just combined. Spoon the mixture into lightly greased muffin pans.

3 Bake at 200°C for 25 minutes or until golden brown.

Makes 12

Oven temperature 200°C, 400°F, Gas 6

Mushroom Muffins

250g plain flour
1 tbsp baking powder
60g fresh mushrooms, chopped
75g cooked brown rice
60g shredded tasty cheese
1 tbsp parsley flakes
2 tsp chives, chopped
125g margarine, melted
1 cup milk
1 egg, beaten

1 Sift flour and baking powder into a large bowl. Mix in mushrooms, rice, cheese and herbs.

2 Make a well in the centre of the dry ingredients. Add the remaining ingredients. Mix until just combined (see note).

3 Spoon the mixture into greased muffin tins until ¾ full. Bake in the oven at 200°C for 25 minutes. Remove from the tin. Cool on a wire rack. Serve hot or cold.

Makes about 12

Note: Don't worry if not all the flour is incorporated as this gives muffins their characteristic texture. 16 strokes is usually enough when mixing.

Oven temperature 200°C, 400°F, Gas 6

Banana Choc-Chip Muffins

1 large ripe banana
1 cup milk
1 egg
60g margarine, melted
180g self-raising flour
125g caster sugar
125g choc bits

1 In a mixing bowl mash the banana and add the milk, egg and margarine. Mix well.

2 Stir the flour, sugar and choc bits into the banana mixture, mixing only until the ingredients are combined.

3 Spoon the mixture into well greased muffin tins. Bake in an oven at 190°C for 20 minutes. Serve warm or cold.

Makes 12

Oven temperature 190°C, 370°F, Gas 5

Blackberry Spice Muffins Photograph opposite

75g self-raising wholemeal flour
60g self-raising flour
1/2 tsp ground allspice
45g brown sugar
60g ground almonds
185g blackberries
1 banana, mashed
1 cup buttermilk
90mL vegetable oil
1 egg, lightly beaten

1 Sift together wholemeal flour, flour and allspice into a bowl. Return husks to bowl. Add sugar, almonds, blackberries and banana and mix to combine.

2 Place buttermilk, oil and egg in a bowl and whisk to combine. Stir milk mixture into dry ingredients and mix until just combined.

3 Spoon mixture into 12 non-stick 125mL capacity muffin tins and bake for 15–20 minutes or until muffins are cooked when tested with a skewer. Turn onto a wire rack to cool.

Makes 12

Note: If buttermilk is unavailable, use equal parts of low-fat natural yoghurt and reduced-fat milk instead.

Oven temperature 190°C, 375°F, Gas 5

Mango Bran Muffins Photograph opposite

125g self-raising flour
2 tsp baking powder
1 tsp ground cardamom
45g oatbran
60g brown sugar
1 mango, chopped
2 egg whites
185mL reduced-fat milk
60mL vegetable oil

1 Sift together flour, baking powder and cardamom into a bowl. Add oatbran, sugar and mango and mix to combine.

2 Place egg whites, milk and oil in a bowl and whisk to combine. Stir milk mixture into flour mixture and mix well to combine.

3 Spoon mixture into 12 non-stick 90mL capacity muffin tins and bake for 15–20 minutes or until muffins are cooked when tested with a skewer. Turn onto a wire rack to cool.

Makes 12

Note: When fresh mangoes are unavailable, drained, canned mangoes can be used instead.

Oven temperature 190°C, 375°F, Gas 5

Apple and Bran Muffins

230g wholemeal self-raising flour
$\frac{1}{2}$ tsp ground nutmeg
$\frac{1}{4}$ tsp baking powder
30g bran cereal, toasted
60g brown sugar
2 green apples, grated
2 eggs, lightly beaten
45g low-fat natural yoghurt
1 tbsp polyunsaturated vegetable oil

1   Sift together flour, nutmeg and baking powder into a bowl. Add bran cereal and sugar and mix to combine.
2   Make a well in the centre of the flour mixture. Add apples, eggs, yoghurt and oil and mix until just combined.
3   Spoon mixture into 12 greased 125mL muffin tins and bake for 15 minutes or until muffins are cooked when tested with a skewer.

Makes 12

Note: The secret to making great muffins is in the mixing – they should be mixed as little as possible. While it doesn't matter if the mixture is lumpy, overmixing results in tough muffins.

Oven temperature 180°C, 350°F, Gas 4

Lemon-Poppy Seed Muffins

2 eggs, lightly beaten
1 cup sour cream
1 cup milk
60mL olive oil
90mL honey
3 tbsp poppy seeds
1 tbsp grated lemon rind
280g self-raising flour, sifted

Lemon Cream-Cheese Icing
60g cream cheese, softened
1 tbsp lemon juice
125g icing sugar

Muffins

1 Place eggs, sour cream, milk, oil, honey, poppy seeds and lemon rind in a bowl and mix well to combine.
2 Add flour to poppy seed mixture and mix until just combined.
3 Spoon mixture into six greased 250mL capacity muffin tins and bake for 25–30 minutes or until muffins are cooked when tested with a skewer. Turn onto wire racks to cool.

Lemon Cream-Cheese Icing

1 Place cream cheese, lemon juice and icing sugar in a food processor and process until smooth. Top cold muffins with icing.

Makes 6

Note: A simple glacé icing is another suitable topping for muffins. To make, sift 155g icing sugar into a bowl, slowly stir in 3 teaspoons of warm water and a few drops of almond or vanilla essence to make a glaze of drizzling consistency. To vary the flavour, omit the essence and substitute the water with 3 teaspoons of citrus juice or a favourite liqueur.

Oven temperature 180°C, 350°F, Gas 4

Banana and Pineapple Muffins Photograph opposite

165g wholemeal self-raising flour
1 tsp baking powder
1 tsp mixed spice
4 tbsp brown sugar
45g oatbran
1 small banana, mashed
150g canned crushed pineapple, drained
3 egg whites, lightly beaten
2 tbsp polyunsaturated oil
1/2 cup pineapple juice

1 Sift flour, baking powder and spice into a mixing bowl. Add sugar and oatbran.

2 Make a well in the centre of the dry ingredients. Combine the banana, pineapple, egg whites, oil and juice. Stir into the flour mixture and mix to combine all ingredients.

3 Spoon mixture into lightly greased muffin pans. Bake at 200°C for 12–15 minutes or until golden brown.

Makes 12

Oven temperature 200°C, 400°F, Gas 6

Orange and Blueberry Muffins

1 orange
1/2 cup orange juice
125g butter, chopped
1 egg
185g plain flour
170g caster sugar
1 tsp bicarbonate of soda
1 tsp baking powder
1/4 teaspoon salt
125g frozen or fresh blueberries

1 Preheat oven to 200°C. Peel the rind from the orange, remove all pith, and cut the rind into small pieces. Remove membrane and seeds from orange and cut the orange into segments.

2 Place orange rind and segments, orange juice, butter and egg in a food processor and process until well combined (mixture will curdle). Transfer mixture to a large bowl.

3 Sift together flour, sugar, bicarbonate of soda, baking powder and salt, add to orange mixture and lightly mix. Batter should be lumpy. Fold in the berries.

4 Divide batter between 12–16 greased 90mL capacity muffin tins, filling 2/3 full. Bake for 18–20 minutes until cooked and golden. Cool on wire racks.

Makes 12–16

Oven temperature 200°C, 400°F, Gas 6

Potato Sour-Cream Muffins

250g mashed potato
2 eggs, lightly beaten
1 cup milk
185g sour cream
60g butter, melted
315g self-raising flour, sifted
3 tbsp snipped fresh chives

1 Place potato in a bowl. Add eggs, milk, sour cream and butter to the bowl and mix well to combine.

2 Combine flour and chives. Add to potato mixture and mix until just combined. Spoon mixture into 6 greased 250mL capacity muffin tins and bake for 25–30 minutes or until muffins are cooked when tested with a skewer. Serve warm or cold.

Makes 6

Note: A properly cooked muffin should have risen well, be slightly domed in the middle (but not peaked) and be evenly browned. It should also shrink slightly from the sides of the tin.

Oven temperature 180°C, 350°F, Gas 4

Cheese and Bacon Muffins

4 rashers bacon, chopped
1 egg, lightly beaten
1 cup milk
60mL vegetable oil
2 tbsp chopped fresh parsley
250g self-raising flour, sifted
90g grated tasty (mature cheddar) cheese

1 Place bacon in a frying pan and cook over a medium heat, stirring, until crisp. Remove bacon from pan and drain on absorbent kitchen paper.

2 Place egg, milk, oil and parsley in a bowl and mix to combine. Combine flour and cheese. Add flour mixture and bacon to egg mixture and mix until combined.

3 Spoon mixture into 12 greased 125mL capacity muffin tins and bake for 20–25 minutes or until muffins are cooked when tested with a skewer. Serve warm or cold.

Makes 12

Note: An accurate oven is essential for successful baking. It should be well insulated and draught-proof, as a discrepancy of a few degrees can ruin baked goods. Regular checking with an oven thermometer helps avoid baking failures.

Oven temperature 180°C, 350°F, Gas 4

Spiced Apple Muffins

200g plain wholemeal flour
1 tbsp baking powder
1 tsp ground mixed spice
pinch of salt
50g light soft brown sugar
1 medium egg, beaten
200mL half-fat milk
50g margarine, melted
1 cooking apple, peeled,
cored and chopped

1   Preheat the oven to 200°C. Line a muffin or deep bun tin with 9 muffin cases and set aside. Place the flour, baking powder, mixed spice and salt in a bowl and mix well.

2   In a separate large bowl, mix together the sugar, egg, milk and margarine, then gently fold in the flour mixture – just enough to combine them. The mixture should look quite lumpy; it will produce heavy muffins if overmixed. Gently fold in the apple.

3   Divide the mixture between the muffin cases. Bake in the oven for 20 minutes or until risen and golden brown. Transfer to a wire rack to cool.

Makes 9

Note: The problem with these muffins is that they smell so good when they come out of the oven, they may not last until tea time! Serve them on their own with a cup of tea.

Oven temperature 200°C, 400°F, Gas 6

Carrot and Sesame Muffins

375g self-raising flour
$^{1}/_{2}$ tsp bicarbonate of soda
1 tsp ground mixed spice
90g brown sugar
1 large carrot, grated
4 tbsp toasted sesame seeds
170g sultanas
200g natural yoghurt
1 cup milk
3 tbsp melted butter
3 egg whites, lightly beaten

1 Sift together flour, bicarbonate of soda and mixed spice into a large bowl. Add sugar, carrot, sesame seeds and sultanas and mix to combine.

2 Place yoghurt, milk, butter and egg whites in a bowl and whisk to combine. Stir yoghurt mixture into flour mixture and mix until just combined. Spoon batter into lightly greased muffin tins and bake for 20 minutes or until golden and cooked.

Makes 24

Note: Delicious light muffins are perfect weekend fare. Any leftovers can be frozen and used when time is short.

Oven temperature 200°C, 400°F, Gas 6

Sticky Date Muffins

250g self-raising flour
1 tsp bicarbonate of soda
1 tsp ground cinnamon
60g brown sugar
90g butter
125g chopped dates
1 egg, lightly beaten
1 cup buttermilk or milk

Brandy Sauce
100g butter
45g brown sugar
1 tbsp golden syrup
1 tbsp brandy (optional)

Muffins

1 Sift flour, bicarbonate of soda and cinnamon together into a bowl. Set aside.

2 Place sugar, butter and dates in a saucepan and heat over a low heat, stirring constantly, until butter melts. Pour date mixture into dry ingredients, add egg and milk. Mix until just combined.

3 Spoon mixture into six greased 250mL capacity muffin tins and bake for 30 minutes or until muffins are cooked when tested with a skewer.

Brandy Sauce

1 Place butter, sugar, golden syrup and brandy (if using) in a saucepan and heat over a low heat, stirring constantly, until sugar dissolves. Bring to the boil, then reduce heat and simmer for 3 minutes or until sauce is thick and syrupy. Serve with warm muffins.

Makes 6

Note: If 250mL capacity muffin tins are unavailable, use the standard 125mL capacity tins and bake for approximately half the recommended time. The yield, of course, will be doubled. These muffins make a delicious dessert treat, but are just as good in lunch boxes and for snacks without the sauce.

Oven temperature 190°C, 375°F, Gas 5

Slices

Your family and friends will be delighted when you open a cake tin that actually contains a selection of homemade slices. The recipes in this chapter are great for morning and afternoon teas and are equally good in packed lunches.

Macadamia Caramel Squares

Base
100g white melting chocolate
125g butter
90g icing sugar
60g macadamia nuts, roasted
and ground
200g plain flour

Topping
400g can sweetened condensed milk
200g milk chocolate
suitable for melting, such as 'melts'
2 large eggs
2 tbsp plain flour
90g shortbread biscuits chopped,
not crushed
200g roasted macadamia nuts
roughly chopped
60g roasted macadamia nuts (extra)

Base
1 Preheat oven to 180°C. Butter a lamington tin 28 x 18cm then line it with baking paper.
2 Melt the white chocolate then add it to a mixer with the butter, icing sugar, crushed macadamia nuts and plain flour.
3 Mix on low speed until all the ingredients are combined, then press the mixture into the prepared tin. Bake for 18 minutes, then cool.

Topping
1 Preheat the oven to 160°C. In a saucepan, heat the condensed milk and milk chocolate together (until the chocolate has melted). Add the eggs, flour, shortbread biscuit pieces and chopped macadamia nuts, and mix gently.
2 Pour this mixture over the base, then sprinkle the extra macadamia nuts over. Bake at 160°C for 40 minutes. Remove from the oven and cool completely in the refrigerator before slicing.

Makes 18

Note: This delicious confection will be adored by adults and children alike. A sure winner for picnics and outdoor entertaining, the brownie–like consistency will keep them coming back for more!

Oven temperature 160°C, 325°F, Gas 3

Lamingtons (Microwave)

175g butter
180g caster sugar
3 eggs
180g self-raising flour
½ tsp baking powder
4 tbsp milk

Chocolate Icing
465g icing sugar
3 tbsp cocoa
2 tbsp butter
5 tbsp water
180g coconut, dessicated

Lamingtons

1   Cream butter and sugar together, add egg and beat well. Sift flour and baking powder together, stir into mixture alternately with milk.

2   Pour into a lightly greased 28 x 18cm, or 22cm square microwave dish.

3   Elevate and cook on power level 9 (High) for 7 minutes. Shield ends with a strip of foil after 4 minutes.

4   Allow to stand for 10 minutes then turn out and allow to cool completely. Cut into 12 even pieces.

Chocolate Icing

1   Place all ingredients except the coconut into a large bowl. Heat on power level 9 (High) for 3 minutes.

2   Stir after 1 minute; at this stage mixture will be stiff, but on further heating it will come to a pouring consistency.

3   Spread coconut onto a sheet of paper. Working quickly, dip cakes one a time into icing, turn to coat both sides, then remove with a fork. Drain off excess icing and toss in coconut.

4   Icing will cool and stiffen after 3 or 4 lamingtons are dipped. Just return to microwave and heat for 20 seconds on high. Repeat process until all 12 are completed.

Makes 12

Hint: To ice party cakes quickly, dip the top of each cake into soft icing, twirl slightly and quickly turn right side up.

Microwave temp: Level 9 (High)

Hot Brownies with White Chocolate Sauce

100g soft margarine, plus extra
for greasing
100g soft dark brown sugar
1 large egg, beaten
1 tbsp golden syrup
1 tbsp cocoa powder, sifted
50g wholemeal self-raising flour, sifted
25g pecan nuts or walnuts, chopped

White Chocolate Sauce
1 tbsp cornflour
200mL full-fat milk
50g white chocolate, broken into
small chunks

Brownies

1 Preheat the oven to 180°C. Grease the sides and base of an 18cm square cake tin. Beat the margarine and sugar in a bowl until pale and creamy, then beat in the egg, syrup, cocoa powder and flour until it forms a thick, smooth batter. Stir in the nuts.

2 Spoon the mixture into the tin, smooth the top and bake for 35–40 minutes, until well risen and just firm to the touch.

White Chocolate Sauce

1 Meanwhile, make the chocolate sauce. Blend the cornflour with 1 tablespoon of the milk. Heat the rest of the milk in a saucepan, add the cornflour mixture, then gently bring to the boil, stirring as the sauce thickens. Cook gently for 1–2 minutes.

2 Add the white chocolate, then remove from the heat and stir until it melts. Cut the brownies into 8 pieces and serve warm with the chocolate sauce.

Note: These brownies are delicious cold, but served straight from the oven with white chocolate sauce spooned over them, they're absolutely fabulous!

Oven temperature 180°C, 350°F, Gas 4

Fruit Slice

Base

180g self-raising flour
2¹/₂ tbsp cornflour
60g ground rice
250g butter or margarine
60g caster sugar
1 egg

Filling

250g dates, chopped
125g sultanas
125g raisins
30g mixed peel
30g glace cherries
1 tbsp butter or margarine
mixed spice, to taste
170g can passionfruit pulp
1 tbsp arrowroot
2 tbsp water
beaten egg and caster sugar
for glazing

Base

1   Sift the flours into a bowl and stir in the ground rice.
2   Rub in the butter or margarine, stir in the sugar and bind together with the egg. Press half the mixture over the base of a buttered and lined lamington tin.

Filling

1   Combine the fruit, butter or margarine, spice and passionfruit in a saucepan and stir over a low heat until the mixture thickens slightly. Blend the arrowroot and water together, stir into the fruit and allow to cook, stirring all the time for 3 minutes.
2   Remove from the heat and cool. Spoon the filling onto the pastry base and top with the remaining pastry, crimping the edges to decorate and seal. Glaze with the beaten egg, sprinkle with sugar and bake at 220°C for 20–25 minutes. Serve warm with custard.

Serves 8–10

Oven temperature 220°C, 440°F, Gas 7

Brandy Apricot Slice

90g dried apricots, chopped
2 tbsp brandy
100g dark chocolate
4 tbsp margarine
3 tbsp milk
1 egg
60g caster sugar
90g plain flour
¼ tsp baking powder

Chocolate Frosting
60g dark chocolate
1 tbsp milk
250g sifted icing sugar
1 tbsp margarine

1 Combine apricots and brandy. Set aside for 15 minutes. Sieve the flour. Melt chocolate and margarine together, stir in milk, egg, sugar and the sifted flour and baking powder. Mix well. Stir apricots through the chocolate mixture.

2 Spoon mixture into a lightly greased 20cm square sandwich pan. Bake in an oven at 180°C for 12–15 minutes or until firm. Cool in the tin. Ice with chocolate frosting.

Chocolate Frosting

1 Melt together chocolate and milk, and blend in icing sugar and margarine. Mix well.

Makes 16

Oven temperature 180°C, 350°F, Gas 4

39

Sticky Chocolate and Raspberry Slice

75g unsalted butter, plus extra
for greasing

75g plain chocolate, broken
into chunks

75g fresh or frozen raspberries, plus
extra to decorate

2 medium eggs, separated

50g caster sugar

25g ground almonds

25g cocoa powder, sifted

25g plain flour,
sifted icing sugar to dust and fresh
mint to decorate

Raspberry Sauce

150g fresh or frozen raspberries

1 tbsp caster sugar (optional)

1   Preheat the oven to 180°C. Grease the base and sides of an 18cm loose-bottomed cake tin and line with baking paper. Melt the butter and chocolate in a bowl set over a saucepan of simmering water, stirring. Cool slightly.

2   Press the raspberries through a sieve. Whisk the egg yolks and sugar until pale and creamy, then mix in the almonds, cocoa, flour, melted chocolate and sieved raspberries.

3   Whisk the egg whites until they form stiff peaks (this is best done with an electric whisk). Fold a little into the chocolate mixture to loosen, then fold in the remainder. Spoon into the tin and cook for 25 minutes or until risen and just firm. Cool for 1 hour.

4   Remove the cake from the tin and dust with the icing sugar. Serve with the sauce, decorated with mint and raspberries.

Raspberry Sauce

1   Sieve the raspberries, then stir in the sugar, if using.

Oven temperature 180°C, 350°F, Gas 4

Chocolate Pecan Fingers

90g dark chocolate
125g margarine
2 tsp instant coffee powder
2 eggs
180g caster sugar
$^1/_2$ tsp vanilla
125g plain flour
90g chopped pecans
icing sugar, for dusting

1   Melt the chocolate and margarine together over hot water, stir in the coffee powder and allow to cool slightly.

2   In a medium sized bowl whisk the eggs until foamy, add the sugar and vanilla.

3   Fold the chocolate mixture through the eggs. Stir in the flour and pecans and mix until just blended. Spoon the mixture into a lightly greased 20cm square cake pan. Bake in an oven at 180°C for 25 minutes or until the cake springs back when touched. Cool in the tin. Dust with sifted icing sugar and cut into fingers to serve.

Makes about 15

Oven temperature 180°C, 350°F, Gas 4

Sultana Oat Slice

4 tbsp margarine
75mL honey
1 packet sultana buttercake
2 eggs
30g rolled oats

Yoghurt Frosting
300g icing sugar, sifted
2 tbsp vanilla yoghurt
4 tbsp toasted shredded coconut

1   In a small saucepan melt the margarine and honey together. Combine the sultana buttercake, eggs and rolled oats, pour the melted ingredients over the buttercake mixture and mix well.

2   Spoon mixture into a lightly greased 20cm square sandwich tin. Bake in an oven at 180°C for 20 minutes or until firm to the touch. Cool before icing with yoghurt frosting, sprinkle with toasted shredded coconut. Cut into squares to serve.

Yoghurt Frosting

1   Mix sugar and vanilla and beat until smooth.

Makes 16 slices

Pistachio Truffles

315g dark chocolate, broken into pieces
45g butter, chopped
$\frac{1}{2}$ cup thickened double cream
2 tbsp sugar
2 tbsp Galliano liqueur
125g chopped pistachio nuts

1 Place chocolate, butter, cream and sugar in a heatproof bowl set over a saucepan of simmering water and heat, stirring, until mixture is smooth. Add liqueur and half the pistachio nuts and mix well to combine. Chill the mixture for 1 hour or until firm enough to roll into balls.

2 Roll tablespoons of the mixture into balls, then roll the balls in the remaining pistachio nuts. Chill until required.

Serves 4

Tip: To bring out the bright green colour of the pistachios, blanch the shelled nuts in boiling water for 30 seconds, drain and vigorously rub in a clean towel to remove their skins.

Caramel-Walnut Petits Fours

250g sugar
90g brown sugar
2 cups thickened double cream
1 cup golden syrup
60g butter, chopped
$\frac{1}{2}$ tsp bicarbonate of soda
155g chopped walnuts
1 tbsp vanilla essence

Chocolate Icing
375g dark or milk chocolate, melted
2 tsp vegetable oil

1 Place sugar, brown sugar, cream, golden syrup and butter in a saucepan and heat over a low heat, stirring constantly, until sugar dissolves. As sugar crystals form on the sides of the pan, brush with a wet pastry brush.

2 Bring the syrup to the boil and stir in the bicarbonate of soda. Reduce heat and simmer until syrup reaches the hard-ball stage or 120°C on a sugar thermometer.

3 Stir in walnuts and vanilla essence and pour mixture into a greased and foil-lined 20cm square cake tin. Set aside at room temperature for 5 hours or until caramel sets.

4 Remove caramel from the tin and cut into 2cm squares.

Chocolate Icing

1 Combine chocolate and oil. Half dip caramels in melted chocolate, place on greaseproof paper and leave to set.

Makes 40

Note: To easily remove the caramel from the tin, let the foil lining overhang the tin on two opposite sides to form handles for lifting.

Fruit Medley Slice

100g margarine
125g self-raising flour
155g brown sugar
90g desiccated coconut

Topping
250g dried fruit medley
4 tbsp orange juice
155g brown sugar
6 tbsp margarine, melted
60g chopped pecans
45g desiccated coconut
100g white chocolate, melted

1 Combine the margarine, flour, brown sugar and coconut. Mix well. Press mixture onto the base of a 30 x 20cm slice tin.

2 Bake in an oven at 180°C for 15 minutes. Remove from the oven and pour the topping over the base. Then return to the oven and cook for a further 15 minutes. Cool in the tin.

3 Decorate top with melted chocolate and cut into squares to serve.

Topping

1 Soak fruit medley in orange juice for 10 minutes. Combine with brown sugar, melted margarine, pecans and coconut. Mix well.

Tip: Keep icing in a bowl covered with a damp cloth to prevent it from drying out and forming a crust.

Oven temperature 180°C, 350°F, Gas 4

46

Baklava

250g unsalted butter, melted
400g blanched roasted almonds, ground
1½ tsp cinnamon
½ cup caster sugar
700g filo pastry

Syrup
3 cups caster sugar
1½ cups water
1 cinnamon stick
1 piece of orange or lemon rind
1 tbsp honey

1 Melt butter, set aside.
2 Mix nuts in a bowl, add cinnamon and sugar.
3 Brush a 25 x 33cm baking tray with the butter. Place 1 sheet of filo on the bottom of the dish with ends hanging over sides. Brush with melted butter and add another layer of filo. Repeat with 8 more filo sheets.
4 Sprinkle nut mixture generously over the filo. Continue the layering of filo pastry (3 sheets) and 1 layer of nuts until all the nuts are used.
5 Top with 8 reserved sheets of filo, making sure the top sheet is well buttered. Cut the top lengthways in parallel strips.
6 Bake in an oven at 275°C for 30 minutes, then reduce the heat to 150°C and bake for a further hour. Pour cold syrup over the baklava and cut it into diamond shapes.

Syrup
1 Place ingredients in saucepan and bring to the boil. Reduce heat and let simmer for 10–15 minutes. Leave to cool before use.

Two-Fruit Crumble Slice

Base
125g sweet biscuits

125g butter

125g brown sugar

100g milk chocolate (suitable for melting, such as 'melts')

75g desiccated coconut

1 tbsp cocoa

Filling
250g dried apricots

250g dried peaches

1 tbsp honey

juice and zest of two oranges

50mL water

Topping
90g shredded coconut

75g rolled oats

90g butter

2 tbsp golden syrup

60g cashew nuts (salted, roasted and chopped)

Base

1 Preheat oven to 180°C and butter a 20cm square cake tin.

2 Using a food processor, crush the sweet biscuits until finely ground.

3 Place the butter, brown sugar and chocolate in a saucepan and heat gently stirring well to avoid burning. When the mixture has melted, add the coconut, biscuit crumbs and cocoa, and stir vigorously until the mixture is well combined. Press evenly into the base of the prepared cake tin and bake for 10 minutes. Cool.

Filling

1 Chop the dried fruit and place in a saucepan with the honey, orange juice and zest and water, and bring to the boil. Simmer for 10 minutes, until the fruit has softened and all the liquid has been absorbed. Allow to cool, then spread over the cooked biscuit base.

Topping

1 Mix the coconut and oats together, cook in the microwave on 'high' for 2 minutes then stir gently. Cook for a further minute or two until deep golden. In a separate bowl or small saucepan, heat the butter and golden syrup together until bubbling, then stir in the oat mixture and cashews, and mix thoroughly until all ingredients are moistened.

2 Sprinkle the topping over the filling to cover it completely, then bake for a further 15–18 minutes until the topping is golden. Remove from the oven and cool, then slice into 16 even pieces.

Makes 16

Note: One of the best sweet choices when entertaining is a slice– usually a fairly flat, cake mixture that has two or three layers of different flavours and textures. Slices are usually made well ahead of time, allowing the cook to enjoy socialising as much as the guests do. Most slices travel well, making them perfect for gifts, picnics and school lunches.

Oven temperature 180°C, 350°F, Gas 4

Strawberry and Chocolate Slice

250g chocolate biscuits
2 tbsp butter
1 tbsp gelatine
60mL water
250g packet cream cheese
300mL thickened cream
150g packet marshmallows
1 punnet strawberries

1 Line a 28 x18cm lamington tin with plastic wrap.

2 Place biscuits into a food processor and process until fine. Combine with melted butter and press into the base of the tin, refrigerate until firm.

3 Sprinkle the gelatine over the water, dissolve over hot water, allow to cool.

4 Place cream cheese into a food processor and process until smooth. Add the cream, gelatine, marshmallows and half the strawberries and process until well mixed.

5 Pour the filling over the biscuit base and decorate with the remaining halved strawberries, chill until firm. Remove the slice from the pan and cut into slices to serve.

Makes 12

Chocolate Panforte

1 cup liquid honey
250g sugar
250g almonds, toasted and chopped
250g hazelnuts, toasted and chopped
125g glacé apricots, chopped
125g glacé peaches, chopped
100g candied mixed peel
185g flour, sifted
45g cocoa powder, sifted
2 tsp ground cinnamon
155g dark chocolate, melted
rice paper

1 Place honey and sugar in a small saucepan and heat, stirring constantly, over a low heat until the sugar dissolves. Bring to the boil, then reduce the heat and simmer, stirring constantly, for 5 minutes or until mixture thickens.

2 Place almonds, hazelnuts, apricots, peaches, mixed peel, flour, cocoa powder and cinnamon in a bowl and mix to combine. Stir in the honey syrup. Add the chocolate and mix well to combine.

3 Line a shallow 18 x 28cm cake tin with rice paper. Pour the mixture into the tin and bake for 20 minutes. Turn onto a wire rack to cool, then cut into small pieces.

Makes 32

Note: Everyone's favourite biscuits is full of the flavour, of fruit, toasted almonds, hazelnuts and a generous portion of chocolate!

Oven temperature 180°C, 350°F, Gas 4

51

Double-Fudge Blondies

250g butter, softened
375g sugar
1 tsp vanilla essence
4 eggs, lightly beaten
225g plain flour
$\frac{1}{2}$ tsp baking powder
185g white chocolate, melted

Cream Cheese Filling
250g cream cheese, softened
60g white chocolate, melted
60mL maple syrup
1 egg
1 tbsp plain flour

Cream Cheese Filling

1 Place cream cheese, chocolate, maple syrup, egg and flour in a bowl and beat until smooth. Set aside.

Blondies

2 Place butter, sugar and vanilla essence in a bowl and beat until light and fluffy. Gradually beat in the eggs.

3 Sift together the flour and baking powder over the butter mixture. Add the chocolate and mix well to combine.

4 Spread half the mixture over the base of a greased and lined 23cm square cake tin. Top with cream cheese filling and then with the remaining mixture. Bake for 40 minutes or until firm. Cool in the tin, then cut into squares.

Makes 24

Note: These lusciously rich white brownies can double as a dessert if drizzled with melted white or dark chocolate and topped with toasted flaked almonds.

Oven temperature 180°C, 350°F, Gas 4

Chocolate Nougat Hearts

375g milk chocolate, broken into pieces
45g butter, chopped
1 cup thickened double cream
200g nougat, chopped
100g almonds, toasted and chopped

1 Place chocolate, butter and cream in a heatproof bowl set over a saucepan of simmering water and heat, stirring, until mixture is smooth.

2 Add nougat and almonds and mix well to combine. Pour mixture into a greased and lined, shallow 18 x 28cm cake tin. Refrigerate for 2 hours or until set.

3 Using a heart-shaped cutter, cut out hearts from the set mixture.

Makes 40

Note: Dip the cutter in warm water and dry on a clean towel between each cut to achieve evenly straight edges.

53

Quick Bakes

Baking has never been simpler or more fun than with this selection of quick and easy cakes and bakes. A bowl, a beater and few minutes in the kitchen is all it takes to fill the house with the homely warmth and aroma that only a homemade scone or loaf of bread can provide. There's a recipe on these pages to please everyone and every occasion. So, discover the pleasure of home baking and watch your friends and family return for more.

Soda Bread Photograph on Page 54

500g plain flour
1 tsp bicarbonate of soda
1 tsp salt
45g butter
2 cups buttermilk or milk

1 Sift together the flour, bicarbonate of soda and salt into a bowl. Rub in the butter, using your fingertips, until the mixture resembles coarse breadcrumbs. Make a well in the centre of the flour mixture, pour in the milk or buttermilk and, using a round-ended knife, mix to form a soft dough.

2 Turn dough onto a floured surface and knead lightly until smooth. Shape into an 18cm round and place on a greased and floured baking tray. Score dough into eighths using a sharp knife. Dust lightly with flour and bake for 35–40 minutes or until the loaf sounds hollow when tapped on the base.

Serves 8

Note: A loaf for when you need bread unexpectedly, soda bread is made with bicarbonate of soda rather than yeast so it needs no rising. Its best eaten slightly warm and is delicious with lashings of treacle or golden syrup.

Oven temperature 200°C, 400°F, Gas 6

Fig Scones Photograph on Page 55

250g self-raising flour
65g sugar
$^3/_4$ tsp salt
125g butter
65g finely chopped dried figs
2 eggs, slightly beaten
milk, for brushing
cinnamon and sugar, for glaze

1 Sift all dry ingredients together. Rub in the butter, add the figs and the egg. Stir with a fork until the mixture forms a soft ball.

2 Roll out onto a lightly floured board about 1cm thick and cut into triangles or rounds. Brush the tops with a little milk, sprinkle with sugar and cinnamon and bake in an oven at 200°C until golden brown, about 15 minutes.

Serves 3–4

Oven temperature 200°C, 400°F, Gas 6

Fresh Strawberry Scones

250g self-raising wholemeal flour
1 tsp baking powder
pinch of salt
60g margarine
30g caster sugar
100g fresh strawberries, chopped
100mL half-fat milk, plus extra for glazing

1 Preheat the oven to 220°C. Put the flour, baking powder and salt in a large bowl and stir to mix. Lightly rub in the margarine until the mixture resembles breadcrumbs.

2 Mix in the sugar and strawberries, then add enough milk to form a soft dough. Turn the dough out onto a floured surface, knead lightly, then carefully roll to a thickness of 2cm.

3 Cut out 12 rounds, using a 5cm pastry cutter, and place on a baking sheet. Brush with milk to glaze. Bake in the oven for 8–10 minutes, until well risen and golden brown. Transfer to a wire rack to cool.

Makes 12

Note: To give these traditional scones a warm, spicy flavour, add a teaspoon of ground cinnamon to the flour at the start of this recipe. Serve with crème fraîche and strawberries.

Oven temperature 220°C, 425°F, Gas 7

Wensleydale and Apple Scones

60g butter, cubed, plus extra
for greasing

200g self-raising flour

1 tsp baking powder

salt

60g fine oatmeal, plus extra
for dusting

1 tsp English mustard powder

1 tsp light muscovado sugar

125g Wensleydale cheese,
cut into 1cm cubes

1 large or 2 small eating apples,
peeled, cored and chopped
into 5mm pieces

4–5 tbsp soured cream or buttermilk,
plus extra for glazing

1 Preheat the oven to 200°C. Grease a baking sheet.
2 Sift the flour, baking powder and a good pinch of salt into a bowl, then stir in the oatmeal, mustard powder and sugar. Rub in the butter using your fingertips until it resembles fine breadcrumbs. Stir in the cheese and apples and bind with just enough soured cream or buttermilk to make a soft but not sticky dough.
3 Roll out the dough on a floured surface to about 2cm thick and stamp out 8 scones, using a 6cm pastry cutter. Without overhandling the dough, press the trimmings together and roll out again to make more scones. Place on the baking sheet, brush the tops with soured cream or buttermilk and lightly dust with oatmeal. Bake for 15 minutes, then cool on a wire rack for a few minutes before serving.

Makes 10 –12

Wensleydale cheese can be replaced with another crumbly, moist table cheese such as Pyengana cheddar (Australian), Romney mature (Australian), Grabetto (Australian), or Barry's bay cheddar (New Zealand). These scones bring together a blend of sweet and savoury. Try them with clotted cream.

Oven temperature 200°C, 400°F, Gas 6

Pumpkin Scones

60g butter
2 tbsp caster sugar
60g cooked, mashed pumpkin
$\frac{1}{2}$ tsp nutmeg
1 egg
$\frac{1}{2}$ cup milk
360g self-raising flour, sifted

1 Cream butter and sugar together well, add pumpkin and nutmeg and mix well.

2 Add the egg, then mix milk in gradually. Stir in the flour and mix to a soft dough.

3 Turn onto a floured board and knead lightly. Pat out to $2\frac{1}{2}$cm thickness. Cut into rounds with a floured scone cutter.

4 Place the scones onto a greased baking tray, 5mm apart and glaze with milk.

5 Bake in a preheated oven at 210°C for 15–20 minutes. Slide onto a wire cooling rack to cool. Serve with butter.

Makes 12

Oven temperature 210°C, 410°F, Gas 6

Hot-Cross Buns

60g skim milk powder
1 cup warm water
75g sugar
90g margarine, melted
$^1/_2$ x 50mg ascorbic acid (Vitamin C) tablet, crushed
14g dried yeast
500g plain flour
1 tsp salt
1 tsp cinnamon, ground
1 tsp mixed spice
1 tbsp gluten powder
$^1/_2$ cup each currants and sultanas
1 tbsp mixed peel

Cross Batter
3 tbsp plain flour
3 tsp caster sugar
water to mix

Bun Glaze
$^1/_2$ cup water
125g granulated sugar

1 Dissolve milk powder in warm water. Add sugar, margarine, ascorbic acid and yeast. Sift the flour, salt, spices and gluten into a large bowl. Pour yeast mixture over dry ingredients, mix well to form a soft dough (add extra warm water if necessary).

2 Knead mixture thoroughly on a floured board for 10 minutes or until smooth.

3 Place dough in a greased bowl, cover with a tea towel and stand in a warm place until mixture doubles in bulk (about 45 minutes). Knead the fruit into the dough. Shape the dough into 16 buns and place then in a well greased deep sided baking dish.

4 Leave the buns in a warm place for a further 15–20 minutes. Pipe crosses on each bun using cross batter. Bake in an oven at 230°C for 15 minutes or until buns sound hollow when tapped underneath. Brush buns with glaze while hot.

Cross Batter

1 Mix together flour and sugar, adding sufficient water to give a cream–like consistency.

Bun Glaze

1 Place water and sugar in a small saucepan, stir over low heat until sugar has dissolved. Simmer for 5 minutes without stirring.

Makes 16

Oven temperature 230°C, 450°F, Gas 8

Blue Cheese and Walnut Damper

315g self-raising flour, sifted
250g blue cheese, crumbled
1 tbsp snipped fresh chives
1 tsp paprika
155g walnuts, chopped
1 cup buttermilk or milk
1 tbsp walnut or vegetable oil
60g grated Parmesan cheese

1 Place flour, blue cheese, chives, paprika and 125g of walnuts in a bowl and mix to combine.

2 Make a well in the centre of flour mixture, add the milk and oil and mix to form a soft dough.

3 Turn the dough onto a lightly floured surface and knead until smooth. Roll into a large ball, flatten slightly and place on a lightly greased baking tray. Sprinkle with the Parmesan cheese and remaining walnuts and bake for 40 minutes or until damper is cooked.

Note: This loaf tastes wonderful served hot with hearty soups or at room temperature as part of a cheese and fruit platter.

Oven temperature 180°C, 350°F, Gas 4

Easy Berry Bread

375g self-raising flour
1$\frac{1}{2}$ tsp ground mixed spice
1 tsp baking powder
1$\frac{1}{2}$ tbsp sugar
30g butter
170mL water
$\frac{1}{2}$ cup milk
200g raspberries
1 tbsp caster sugar
4 tsp milk

1 Sift flour, mixed spice and baking powder together into a bowl. Add sugar then, using your fingertips, rub in the butter until the mixture resembles coarse breadcrumbs.

2 Make a well in the centre of the flour mixture and, using a round-ended knife, mix in the water and milk and mix to form a soft dough.

3 Turn the dough onto a floured surface and knead lightly until smooth. Divide the dough into 2 equal portions and flatten each into an 18cm round.

4 Sprinkle raspberries and sugar over the surface of 1 round leaving 2$\frac{1}{2}$ cm around the edge. Brush the edge with a little milk and place the remaining round on top. Seal edges securely using your fingertips.

5 Place loaf on a greased and lightly floured baking tray. Brush surface of loaf with a little milk and bake for 10 minutes at 220°C. Reduce the oven temperature to 180°C and bake for 20–25 minutes longer or until cooked.

Makes one

Note: Butter absorbs other smells easily, so when keeping it in the refrigerator, ensure it's covered and away from foods such as onions and fish or you'll have a strong-smelling butter that will affect the taste of baked goods.

Oven temperature 220°C, 440°F, Gas 7

Shortbread

200g butter, softened
100g caster sugar
1 tsp vanilla essence
280g flour, sifted
60g rice flour (ground rice), sifted

1 Place butter, sugar and vanilla essence in a bowl and beat until light and fluffy. Add flour and rice flour (ground rice) and mix to combine.

2 Roll out the dough on a lightly floured surface to form a 2cm thick circle.

3 Pinch the edges or press the dough into a large shortbread mould. Place on a lightly greased baking tray and bake for 25 minutes or until lightly browned.

Makes 1

Note: Butter shortbread originated in Scotland as a festive confection particularly for Christmas and Hogmanay.

Oven temperature 160°C, 325°F, Gas 3

Cornbread

125g sifted plain flour
4 tsp baking powder
³/₄ tsp salt
30g sugar
125g yellow cornmeal
2 eggs
1 cup milk
30g butter, melted
extra butter, to serve

1 Sift flour with baking powder and salt. Stir in the sugar and cornmeal. Add the eggs, milk and melted butter. Beat until just smooth.

2 Pour into a 23 x 23 x 5cm tin lined with baking paper and bake at 220°C in an oven for 20–25 minutes.

3 Remove from the tin and cut into squares. Serve with butter.

Serves 4

Oven temperature 220°C, 425°F, Gas 7

Mini Savoury Croissants

250g prepared puff pastry
1 egg, lightly beaten with
1 tbsp water
60g Gruyère cheese, grated
4 stalks fresh asparagus, blanched
and finely chopped
$\frac{1}{4}$ tsp paprika
freshly ground black pepper

1 To make filling, place cheese, asparagus, paprika and black pepper to taste in a bowl and mix to combine.
2 Roll out pastry to 30mm thick and cut into 10cm wide strips. Cut each strip into triangles with 10cm bases.
3 Place a little filling across the base of each triangle, roll up from the base and mould into a croissant shape. Brush with egg mixture.
4 Place croissants on greased baking trays and bake for 12–15 minutes or until puffed and golden. Serve hot or cold.

Ham and Cheese Croissants

1 Melt 15g butter in a frying pan and cook 100g finely chopped ham and 2 finely chopped spring onions over a medium heat for 3–4 minutes or until onions are soft. Remove from heat, stir in 2 teaspoons finely chopped parsley and black pepper to taste. Cool. Assemble, sprinkling filling with 45g tasty (mature cheddar) cheese and cook as directed.

Chocolate Croissants

1 Chocolate croissants: Use 45g grated milk or dark chocolate to fill triangles. Assemble and cook as directed.

Makes 12

Note: Puff pastry always gives a spectacular result and no more so than in these mini croissants. The secret with these savoury delights is in the shape. Follow the step-by-step instructions to make the quickest and tastiest treats ever.

Cheesy Herb Bread

250g self-raising flour, sifted
1 tsp salt
1 tsp chicken stock powder
2 tbsp chopped fresh rosemary or
1 tsp dried rosemary
2 tbsp chopped fresh dill
2 tbsp snipped fresh chives
2 tbsp chopped fresh sage or
1 tsp dried sage
185g grated tasty (mature cheddar) cheese
1 egg, lightly beaten
155mL milk
30g butter, melted

1 Place the flour, salt, stock powder, rosemary, dill, chives, sage and 125g of the cheese in a bowl and mix to combine.

2 Combine egg, milk and butter. Add the egg mixture to the dry ingredients and mix to combine.

3 Spoon mixture into a greased and lined 11 x 21cm loaf tin, sprinkle with remaining cheese and bake for 45 minutes or until cooked when tested with a skewer. Turn onto a wire rack to cool.

Makes one 11 x 21cm loaf

Note: Another time, try combining the flavours of thyme, bay leaves and fennel seeds with the rosemary and sage for a loaf infused with the classic 'herbes de Provence'.

Oven temperature 190°C, 370°F, Gas 5

Scones

250g self-raising flour
1 tsp baking powder
2 tbsp sugar
45g butter
1 egg
1/2 cup milk

1　Sift together the flour and baking powder into a large bowl. Stir in the sugar, then rub in butter, using your fingertips, until mixture resembles coarse breadcrumbs.

2　Whisk together egg and milk. Make a well in the centre of the flour mixture, pour in the egg mixture and mix to form a soft dough. Turn onto a lightly floured surface and knead lightly.

3　Press dough out to a 2cm thickness, using the palm of your hand. Cut out scones using a floured 5cm cutter. Avoid twisting the cutter, or the scones will rise unevenly.

4　Arrange scones close together on a greased and lightly floured baking tray or in a shallow 20cm round cake tin. Brush with a little milk and bake for 12–15 minutes or until golden.

Makes 12

Note: To grease and flour a cake tin or baking tray, lightly brush with melted butter or margarine, then sprinkle with flour and shake to coat evenly. Invert on a work surface and tap gently to remove excess flour.

Oven temperature 220°C, 425°F, Gas 7

Potato Scones

185g plain flour
1 tsp baking powder
1/2 teaspoon salt
125g margarine
2 eggs, beaten
100mL milk
125g cold, finely mashed potato
3 shallots, finely chopped
ground black pepper
plain flour, for kneading
butter, for spreading

1 Sift the flour, baking powder and salt together, then rub in the margarine. Beat the eggs and milk together and add to the flour mixture to make a firm dough.

2 Add the potatoes, shallots and pepper. Stir through lightly. Turn onto a floured board or sheet of non-stick oven paper, knead, then roll out to 1cm thickness. Cut into rounds and bake at 230°C in an oven for 30 minutes. Split open while hot and spread with butter to serve.

Serves 6–8

Oven temperature 230°C, 450°F, Gas 8

Cheese and Onion Scones

500g self-raising flour
1 tsp salt
$\frac{1}{4}$ tsp cayenne pepper
60g margarine or butter
100g grated cheese
1 tbsp finely chopped parsley
1 tbsp finely chopped onion
1 egg, beaten
1$\frac{1}{2}$ cups milk

1 Sift flour, salt and cayenne. Rub the margarine or butter into the flour. Add cheese, parsley and onion and mix well.

2 Make a well in the centre and add beaten egg and milk all at once, and mix quickly to a soft dough. Turn out on a floured board and knead just enough to make a smooth surface.

3 Roll to 1cm thickness and cut into rounds. Place on a floured tray, glaze tops with milk or beaten egg and milk. Bake at 230°C in an oven for 10–15 minutes or until scones are browned.

Serves 6

Oven temperature 230°C, 450°F, Gas 8

Fresh Herb and Oat Scones

185g self-raising flour, sifted
45g instant oats
1/2 tsp baking powder
30g margarine
2 tsp chopped fresh parsley
2 tsp chopped fresh basil
2 tsp chopped fresh rosemary
190mL skim milk

1 Place flour, oats and baking powder in a bowl. Rub through the margarine until the mixture resembles fine breadcrumbs. Stir in the parsley, basil and rosemary.

2 Make a well in the centre of the mixture and pour in the milk. Mix lightly with a knife until all ingredients are just combined. Turn mixture out onto a lightly floured board and knead lightly.

3 Press dough out evenly to 2cm thickness. Cut into rounds using a 5cm cutter dipped in flour. Arrange scones side by side in a lightly greased 18cm round shallow cake pan. Brush tops with a little extra milk and bake at 220°C for 15–20 minutes or until scones are golden brown.

Makes 9

Make these delicious scones in advance. Freeze and reheat them just before serving.

Oven temperature 220°C, 440°F, Gas 7

Cheese and Bacon Damper

3 tbsp margarine or butter
310g self-raising flour
2 tsp parsley flakes
1 tsp chopped chives
125g grated tasty (mature cheddar) cheese
2 rashers cooked bacon, finely chopped
1 egg
185mL milk

1 Rub the margarine or butter into the flour until the mixture resembles coarse breadcrumbs.
2 Stir in the parsley, chives, cheese and bacon, mix well.
3 Combine the egg and milk, stir into the dry ingredients and mix to a soft dough.
4 Turn dough onto a lightly floured board and knead lightly.
5 Shape into a cob, cut a deep cross in the centre and place on a sheet of baking paper on an oven tray.
6 Bake in the oven at 200°C for 30 minutes or until hollow-sounding when tapped underneath.
7 Serve hot with a crock of butter on a buffet table, cut into small pieces.

Serves 6–8

Oven temperature 200°C, 400°F, Gas 6

Olive Soda Bread

125g butter, softened
60g sugar
1 egg
470g wholemeal self-raising flour
185g plain flour
1 1/2 tsp bicarbonate of soda
1 1/2 cups buttermilk or milk
125g black olives, chopped
2 tsp fennel seeds
1 tsp coarse sea salt

1 Place butter, sugar and egg in a food processor and process until smooth. Add wholemeal flour, flour, bicarbonate of soda and milk and process to form a soft dough.

2 Turn the dough onto a lightly floured surface and knead in the olives. Shape the dough into a 20cm round and place on a lightly greased and floured baking tray. Using a sharp knife, cut a cross in the top. Sprinkle with fennel seeds and salt and bake for 45 minutes or until cooked.

Makes one 20cm round loaf

Note: The famous Irish soda bread is influenced here by the Mediterranean flavours of fennel and olives. You can also use one of the many types of marinated olives available.

Oven temperature 200°C, 400°F, Gas 5

Basil-Beer Bread

375g self-raising flour, sifted
60g sugar
6 tbsp chopped fresh basil
1 tsp crushed black peppercorns
1 1/2 cups beer, at room temperature

1 Place flour, sugar, basil, peppercorns and beer in a bowl and mix to make a soft dough.

2 Place dough in a greased and lined 11 x 21cm loaf tin and bake for 50 minutes or until bread is cooked when tested with a skewer.

3 Stand bread in the tin for 5 minutes before turning onto a wire rack to cool. Serve warm or cold.

Makes one 11 x 21cm loaf

Note: This bread is delicious spread with olive or sun-dried tomato paste. Any beer may be used; you can experiment with light and dark ales and even stout to achieve different results.

Oven temperature 160°C, 325°F, Gas 3

Glossary

Acidulated water: water with added acid, such as lemon juice or vinegar, which prevents discolouration of ingredients, particularly fruit or vegetables. The proportion of acid to water is 1 teaspoon per 300mL.

Al dente: Italian cooking term for ingredients that are cooked until tender but still firm to the bite; usually applied to pasta.

Americaine: method of serving seafood, usually lobster and monkfish, in a sauce flavoured with olive oil, aromatic herbs, tomatoes, white wine, fish stock, brandy and tarragon.

Anglaise: cooking style for simple cooked dishes such as boiled vegetables. Assiette anglaise is a plate of cold cooked meats.

Antipasto: Italian for 'before the meal', it denotes an assortment of cold meats, vegetables and cheeses, often marinated, served as an hors d'oeuvre. A typical antipasto might include salami, prosciutto, marinated artichoke hearts, anchovy fillets, olives, tuna fish and Provolone cheese.

Au gratin: food sprinkled with breadcrumbs, often covered with cheese sauce and browned until a crisp coating forms.

Bain marie: a saucepan standing in a large pan which is filled with boiling water to keep liquids at simmering point. A double boiler will do the same job.

Balsamic vinegar: a mild, extremely fragrant, wine-based vinegar made in northern Italy. Traditionally, the vinegar is aged for at least seven years in a series of casks made of various woods.

Baste: to moisten food while it is cooking by spooning or brushing on liquid or fat.

Beat: to stir thoroughly and vigorously.

Beurre manie: equal quantities of butter and flour kneaded together and added, a little at a time, to thicken a stew or casserole.

Bird: see paupiette.

Blanc: a cooking liquid made by adding flour and lemon juice to water in order to keep certain vegetables from discolouring as they cook.

Blanch: to plunge into boiling water and then, in some cases, into cold water. Fruits and nuts are blanched to remove skin easily.

Blanquette: a white stew of lamb, veal or chicken, bound with egg yolks and cream and accompanied by onion and mushrooms.

Blend: to mix thoroughly.

Bonne femme: dishes cooked in the traditional French 'housewife' style. Chicken and pork bonne femme are garnished with bacon, potatoes and baby onion; fish bonne femme with mushrooms in a white wine sauce.

Bouquet garni: a bunch of herbs, usually consisting of sprigs of parsley, thyme, marjoram, rosemary, a bay leaf, peppercorns and cloves, tied in muslin and used to flavour stews and casseroles.

Braise: to cook whole or large pieces of poultry, game, fish, meat or vegetables in a small amount of wine, stock or other liquid in a closed pot. Often the main ingredient is first browned in fat and then cooked in a low oven or very slowly on top of the stove. Braising suits tough meats and older birds and produces a mellow, rich sauce.

Broil: the American term for grilling food.

Brown: cook in a small amount of fat until brown.

Burghul (also bulgur): a type of cracked wheat, where the kernels are steamed and dried before being crushed.

Buttered: to spread with softened or melted butter.

Butterfly: to slit a piece of food in half horizontally, cutting it almost through so that, when opened, it resembles butterfly wings. Chops, large prawns and thick fish fillets are often butterflied so that they cook more quickly.

Buttermilk: a tangy, low-fat cultured milk product; its slight acidity makes it an ideal marinade base for poultry.

Calzone: a semicircular pocket of pizza dough, stuffed with meat or vegetables, sealed and baked.

Caramelise: to melt sugar until it is a golden brown syrup.

Champignons: small mushrooms, usually canned.

Chasseur: French for 'hunter'; a French cooking style in which meat and chicken dishes are cooked with mushrooms, spring onions, white wine and often tomato.

Clarify: to melt butter and drain the oil off the sediment.

Coat: to cover with a thin layer of flour, sugar, nuts, crumbs, poppy or sesame seeds, cinnamon sugar or a few of the ground spices.

Concasser: to chop coarsely, usually tomatoes.

Confit: from the French verb *confire*, meaning to preserve. Food that is made into a preserve by cooking very slowly and thoroughly until tender. In the case of meat, such as duck or goose, it is cooked in its own fat, and covered with the fat so that the meat does not come into contact with the air. Vegetables such as onions are good in confit.

Consommé: a clear soup usually made from beef.

Coulis: a thin puree, usually of fresh or cooked fruit or vegetables, which is soft enough to pour (*couler* means 'to run'). A coulis may be rough-textured or very smooth.

Court bouillon: the liquid in which fish, poultry or meat is cooked. It usually consists of water with bay leaf, onion, carrots and salt and freshly ground black pepper to taste. Other additives may include wine, vinegar, stock, garlic or spring (green) onions.

Couscous: cereal processed from semolina into pellets, traditionally steamed and served with meat and vegetables in the classic North African stew of the same name.

Cream: to make soft, smooth and creamy by rubbing with the back of a spoon or by beating with a mixer. Usually applied to fat and sugar.

Croutons: small toasted or fried cubes of bread.

Cruciferous vegetables: certain members of the mustard, cabbage and turnip families with cross-shaped flowers and strong aromas and flavours.

Crudités: raw vegetables, cut in slices or sticks to nibble plain or with a dipping sauce, or shredded vegetables tossed as salad with a simple dressing.

Cube: to cut into small pieces with six equal sides.

Curdle: to cause milk or sauce to separate into solid and liquid. Example, overcooked egg mixtures.

Daikon radish (also called mooli): a long white Japanese radish.

Dark sesame oil (also called Oriental sesame oil): dark polyunsaturated oil with a low burning point, used for seasoning. Do not replace with lighter sesame oil.

Deglaze: to dissolve congealed cooking juices or glaze on the bottom of a pan by adding a liquid, then scraping and stirring vigorously whilst bringing the liquid to the boil. Juices may be used to make gravy or to add to sauce.

Degrease: to skim grease from the surface of liquid. If possible the liquid should be chilled so the fat solidifies. If not, skim off most of the fat with a large metal spoon, then trail strips of paper towel on the surface of the liquid to remove any remaining globules.

Devilled: a dish or sauce that is highly seasoned with a hot ingredient such as mustard, Worcestershire sauce or cayenne pepper.

Dice: to cut into small cubes.

Dietary fibre: a plant-cell material that is undigested or only partially digested in the human body, but which promotes healthy digestion of other food matter.

Dissolve: mix a dry ingredient with liquid until absorbed.

Dredge: to coat with a dry ingredient, as flour or sugar.

Drizzle: to pour in a fine thread-like stream over a surface.

Dust: to sprinkle or coat lightly with flour or icing sugar.

Dutch oven: a heavy casserole with a lid usually made from cast iron or pottery.

Emulsion: a mixture of two liquids that are not mutually soluble; for example, oil and water.

Entree: in Europe, the 'entry' or hors d'oeuvre; in North America entree means the main course.

Fenugreek: a small, slender annual herb of the pea family. The seeds are spice. Ground fenugreek has a strong maple sweetness, spicy but bitter flavour and an aroma of burnt sugar.

Fillet: special cut of beef, lamb, pork or veal; breast of poultry and game; fish cut off the bone lengthways.

Flake: to break into small pieces with a fork.

Flame: to ignite warmed alcohol over food.

Fold in: a gentle, careful combining of a light or delicate mixture with a heavier mixture, using a metal spoon.

Fricassee: a dish in which poultry, fish or vegetables are bound together with a white or veloute sauce. In Britain and the United States, the name applies to an old-fashioned dish of chicken in a creamy sauce.

Galangal: A member of the ginger family, commonly known as Laos or Siamese ginger. It has a peppery taste with overtones of ginger.

Galette: sweet or savoury mixture shaped as a flat round.

Garnish: to decorate food, usually with something edible.

Gastrique: caramelised sugar deglazed with vinegar and used in fruit-flavoured savoury sauces, in such dishes as duck with orange.

Glaze: a thin coating of beaten egg, syrup or aspic which is brushed over pastry, fruits or cooked meats.

Gluten: a protein in flour that is developed when dough is kneaded, making the dough elastic.

Gratin: a dish cooked in the oven or under the grill so that it develops a brown crust. Breadcrumbs or cheese may be sprinkled on top first. Shallow gratin dishes ensure a maximum area of crust.

Grease: to rub or brush lightly with oil or fat.

Infuse: to immerse herbs, spices or other flavourings in hot liquid to flavour it. Infusion takes from 2–5 minutes depending on the flavouring. The liquid should be very hot but not boiling.

Jardinière: a garnish of garden vegetables, typically carrots, pickling onions, French beans and turnips.

Joint: to cut poultry, game or small animals into serving pieces by dividing at the joint.

Julienne: to cut food into match-like strips.

Lights: lungs of an animal, used in various meat preparations such as pates and faggots.

Line: to cover the inside of a container with paper, to protect or aid in removing mixture.

Knead: to work dough using heel of hand with a pressing motion, while stretching and folding the dough.

Macerate: to soak food in liquid to soften.

Marinade: a seasoned liquid, usually an oil and acid mixture, in which meats or other foods are soaked to soften and give more flavour.

Marinara: Italian 'sailor's style' cooking that does not apply to any particular combination of ingredients. Marinara tomato sauce for pasta is the most familiar.

Marinate: to let food stand in a marinade to season and tenderise.

Mask: to cover cooked food with sauce.

Melt: to heat until liquified.

Mince: to grind into very small pieces.

Mix: to combine ingredients by stirring.

Monounsaturated fats: one of three types of fats found in foods. Are believed not to raise the level of cholesterol in the blood.

Niçoise: a garnish of tomatoes, garlic and black olives; a salad with anchovy, tuna and French beans is typical.

Noisette: small 'nut' of lamb cut from boned loin or rack that is rolled, tied and cut in neat slices. Noisette also means flavoured with hazelnuts, or butter cooked to a nut brown colour.

Non-reactive pan: a cooking pan whose surface does not chemically react with food. Materials used include stainless steel, enamel, glass and some alloys.

Normande: a cooking style for fish, with a garnish of prawn, mussels and mushrooms in a white wine cream sauce; for poultry and meat, a sauce with cream, calvados and apple.

Olive oil: various grades of oil extracted from olives. Extra virgin olive oil has a full, fruity flavour and the lowest acidity. Virgin olive oil is slightly higher in acidity and lighter in flavour. Pure olive oil is a processed blend of olive oils and has the highest acidity and lightest taste.

Panade: a mixture for binding stuffings and dumplings, notably quenelles, often of choux pastry or simply breadcrumbs. A panade may also be made of frangipane, pureed potatoes or rice.

Papillote: to cook food in oiled or buttered greasepoof paper or aluminum foil. Also a decorative frill to cover bone ends of chops and poultry drumsticks.

Parboil: to boil or simmer until part cooked (i.e. cooked further than when blanching).

Pare: to cut away outside covering.

Pate: a paste of meat or seafood used as a spread for toast or crackers.

Paupiette: a thin slice of meat, poultry or fish spread with a savoury stuffing and rolled. In the United States this is also called 'bird' and in Britain an 'olive'.

Peel: to strip away outside covering.

Plump: to soak in liquid or moisten thoroughly until full and round.

Poach: to simmer gently in enough hot liquid to cover, using care to retain shape of food.

Polyunsaturated fat: one of the three types of fats found in food. These exist in large quantities in such vegetable oils as safflower, sunflower, corn and soya bean. These fats lower the level of cholesterol in the blood.

Puree: a smooth paste, usually of vegetables or fruits, made by putting foods through a sieve, food mill or liquefying in a blender or food processor.

Ragout: traditionally a well seasoned, rich stew containing meat, vegetables and wine. Nowadays, a term applied to any stewed mixture.

Ramekins: small oval or round individual baking dishes.

Reconstitute: to put moisture back into dehydrated foods by soaking in liquid.

Reduce: to cook over a very high heat, uncovered, until the liquid is reduced by evaporation.

Refresh: to cool hot food quickly, either under running water or by plunging it into iced water, to stop it cooking. Particularly for vegetables and occasionally for shellfish.

Rice vinegar: mild, fragrant vinegar that is less sweet than cider vinegar and not as harsh as distilled malt vinegar. Japanese rice vinegar is milder than the Chinese variety.

Roulade: a piece of meat, usually pork or veal, that is spread with stuffing, rolled and often braised or poached. A roulade may also be a sweet or savoury mixture that is baked in a Swiss roll tin or paper case, filled with a contrasting filling, and rolled.

Roux: A binding for sauces, made with flour and butter or another fatty substance, to which hot liquid is added. A roux-based sauce may be white, blond or brown, depending on how the butter has been cooked.

Rubbing-in: a method of incorporating fat into flour, by use of fingertips only. Also incorporates air into mixture.

Safflower oil: the vegetable oil that contains the highest proportion of polyunsaturated fats.

Salsa: a juice derived from the main ingredient being cooked, or a sauce added to a dish to enhance its flavour. In Italy the term is often used for pasta sauces; in Mexico the name usually applies to uncooked sauces served as an accompaniment, especially to corn chips.

Saturated fats: one of the three types of fats found in foods. These exist in large quantities in animal products, coconut and palm oils; they raise the level of cholesterol in the blood. As high cholesterol levels may cause heart disease, saturated fat consumption is recommended to be less than 15 percent of calories provided by the daily diet.

Sauté: to cook or brown in small amount of hot fat.

Scald: to bring just to boiling point, usually for milk. Also to rinse with boiling water.

School prawns: delicious eaten just on their own. Smaller prawn than bay, tiger or king. They have a mild flavour, low oiliness and high moisture content, they make excellent cocktails.

Score: to mark food with cuts, notches or lines to prevent curling or to make food more attractive.

Sear: to brown surface quickly over high heat in hot dish.

Seasoned flour: flour with salt and pepper added.

Sift: to shake a dry, powdered substance through a sieve or sifter to remove any lumps and give lightness.

Simmer: to cook food gently in liquid that bubbles steadily just below boiling point so that the food cooks in even heat without breaking up.

Singe: to quickly flame poultry to remove all traces of feathers after plucking.

Skim: to remove a surface layer (often of impurities and scum) from a liquid with a metal spoon or small ladle.

Slivered: sliced in long, thin pieces, usually refers to nuts, especially almonds.

Soften: example: gelatine – sprinkle over cold water and allow to gel (soften) then dissolve and liquefy.

Souse: to cover food, particularly fish, in wine vinegar and spices and cook slowly; the food is cooled in the same liquid. Sousing gives food a pickled flavour.

Steep: to soak in warm or cold liquid in order to soften food and draw out strong flavours or impurities.

Stir-fry: to cook thin slices of meat and vegetable over a high heat in a small amount of oil, stirring constantly to even cooking in a short time. Traditionally cooked in a wok; however, a heavy-based frying pan may be used.

Stock: a liquid containing flavours, extracts and nutrients of bones, meat, fish or vegetables.

Stud: to adorn with; for example, baked ham studded with whole cloves.

Sugo: an Italian sauce made from the liquid or juice extracted from fruit or meat during cooking.

Sweat: to cook sliced or chopped food, usually vegetables, in a little fat and no liquid over very low heat. Foil is pressed on top so that the food steams in its own juices, usually before being added to other dishes.

Thicken: to make a thin, smooth paste by mixing together arrowroot, cornflour or flour with an equal amount of cold water; stir into hot liquid, cook, stirring until thickened.

Timbale: a creamy mixture of vegetables or meat baked in a mould. French for 'kettledrum'; also denotes a drum-shaped baking dish.

Toss: to gently mix ingredients with two forks or fork and spoon.

total fat: the individual daily intake of all three fats previously described in this glossary. Nutritionists recommend that fats provide no more than 35 percent of the energy in the diet.

Vine leaves: tender, lightly flavoured leaves of the grapevine, used in ethnic cuisine as wrappers for savoury mixtures. As the leaves are usually packed in brine, they should be well rinsed before use.

Whip: to beat rapidly, incorporate air and produce expansion.

Zest: thin outer layer of citrus fruits containing the aromatic citrus oil. It is usually thinly pared with a vegetable peeler, or grated with a zester or grater to separate it from the bitter white pith underneath.

Weights and Measures

Cooking is not an exact science; one does not require finely calibrated scales, pipettes and scientific equipment to cook, yet the conversion to metric measures in some countries and its interpretations must have intimidated many a good cook.

In the recipes weights are given for ingredients such, as meats, fish, poultry and some vegetables, but in normal cooking a few ounces or grams one way or another will not affect the success of your dish.

Although recipes have been tested using the Australian Standard 250mL cup, 20mL tablespoon and 5mL teaspoon, they will work just as well with the US and Canadian 8fl oz cup, or the UK 300mL cup. We have used graduated cup measures in preference to tablespoon measures so that proportions are always the same. Where tablespoon measures have been given, they are not crucial measures, so using the smaller tablespoon of the US or UK will not affect the recipe's success. At least we all agree on the teaspoon size.

For breads, cakes and pastries, the only area which might cause concern is where eggs are used, as proportions will then vary. If working with a 250mL or 300mL cup, use large eggs (65g/2$\frac{1}{4}$oz), adding a little more liquid to the recipe for 300mL cup measures if it seems necessary. Use the medium-sized eggs (55g/2oz) with 8fl oz cup measure. A graduated set of measuring cups and spoons is recommended, the cups in particular for measuring dry ingredients. Remember to level such ingredients to ensure an accurate quantity.

English Measures
All measurements are similar to Australian with two exceptions: the English cup measures 300mL/10$\frac{1}{2}$ fl oz, whereas the American and Australian cup measure 250mL/8$\frac{3}{4}$fl oz. The English tablespoon (the Australian dessertspoon) measures 14.8mL /$\frac{1}{2}$ fl oz against Australian tablespoon of 20mL/$\frac{3}{4}$fl oz. The Imperial measurement is 20fl oz to the pint, 40fl oz a quart and 160fl oz one gallon.

American Measures
The American reputed pint is 16fl oz, a quart is equal to 32fl oz and the American gallon, 128fl oz. The American tablespoon is equal to 14.8mL/$\frac{1}{2}$ fl oz, the teaspoon is 5mL/$\frac{1}{6}$ fl oz. The cup measure is 250 mL/8$\frac{3}{4}$ fl oz.

Dry Measures
All the measures are level, so when you have filled a cup or spoon, level it off with the edge of a knife. The scale below is the 'cook's equivalent'; it is not an exact conversion of metric to imperial measurement. To calculate the exact metric equivalent yourself, multiply onces x 28.349523 to obtain grams, or divide 28.349523 grams to obtain onces.

Metric grams (g), kilograms (kg)	Imperial ounces (oz), pound (lb)
15g	$\frac{1}{2}$oz
20g	$\frac{1}{3}$oz
30g	1oz
55g	2oz
85g	3oz
115g	4oz/$\frac{1}{4}$ lb
125g	4$\frac{1}{2}$oz
140/145g	5oz
170g	6oz
200g	7oz
225g	8oz/$\frac{1}{2}$ lb
315g	11oz
340g	12oz/$\frac{3}{4}$ lb
370g	13oz
400g	14oz
425g	15oz
455g	16oz/1 lb
1,000g/1kg	35.3oz/2.2 lb
1.5kg	3.33 lb

Oven Temperatures
The Celsius temperatures given here are not exact; they have been rounded off and are given as a guide only. Follow the manufacturer's temperature guide, relating it to oven description given in the recipe. Remember gas ovens are hottest at the top, electric ovens at the bottom and convection-fan forced ovens are usually even throughout. We included Regulo numbers for gas cookers which may assist. To convert °C to °F multiply °C by 9 and divide by 5 then add 32.

	C°	F°	Gas regulo
Very slow	120	250	1
Slow	150	300	2
Moderately slow	160	325	3
Moderate	180	350	4
Moderately hot	190–200	370–400	5–6
Hot	210–220	410–440	6–7
Very hot	230	450	8
Super hot	250–290	475–500	9–10

Cup Measurements
One cup is equal to the following weights.

	Metric	Imperial
Almonds, flaked	85g	3oz
Almonds, slivered, ground	125g	4½oz
Almonds, kernel	155g	5½oz
Apples, dried, chopped	125g	4½oz
Apricots, dried, chopped	190g	6¾oz
Breadcrumbs, packet	125g	4½oz
Breadcrumbs, soft	55g	2oz
Cheese, grated	115g	4oz
Choc bits	155½g	5oz
Coconut, desiccated	90g	3oz
Cornflakes	30g	1oz
Currants	155½g	5oz
Flour	115g	4oz
Fruit, dried (mixed, sultanas etc)	170g	6 oz
Ginger, crystallised, glace	250g	8oz
Honey, treacle, golden syrup	315g	11oz
Mixed peel	225g	8oz
Nuts, chopped	115g	4oz
Prunes, chopped	225g	8oz
Rice, cooked	155g	5½oz
Rice, uncooked	225g	8oz
Rolled oats	90g	3oz
Sesame seeds	115g	4oz
Shortening (butter, margarine)	225g	8oz
Sugar, brown	155g	5½oz
Sugar, granulated or caster	225g	8oz
Sugar, sifted icing	155g	5½oz
Wheatgerm	60g	2oz

Length
Some of us still have trouble converting imperial length to metric. In this scale, measures have been rounded off to the easiest-to-use and most acceptable figures. To obtain the exact metric equivalent in converting inches to centimetres, multiply inches by 2.54 whereby 1 inch equals 25.4 millimetres and 1 millimetre equals 0.03937 inches.

Cake Dish Sizes

Metric	15cm	18cm	20cm	23cm
Imperial	6in	7in	8in	9in

Loaf Dish Sizes

Metric	23 x 12cm	25 x 8cm	28 x 18cm
Imperial	9 x 5in	10 x 3in	11 x 7in

Liquid Measures

Metric millilitres (mL)	Imperial fluid ounce (fl oz)	Cup and Spoon
5mL	⅙ fl oz	1 teaspoon
20mL	⅔ fl oz	1 tablespoon
30mL	1 fl oz	1 tbsp + 2 tsp
55mL	2 fl oz	
63mL	2¼ fl oz	¼ cup
85mL	3 fl oz	
115mL	4 fl oz	
125mL	4½ fl oz	½ cup
150mL	5¼ fl oz	
188mL	6⅔ fl oz	¾ cup
225mL	8 fl oz	
250mL	8¾ fl oz	1 cup
300mL	10½ fl oz	
370mL	13 fl oz	
400mL	14 fl oz	
438mL	15½ fl oz	1¾ cups
455mL	16 fl oz	
500mL	17½ fl oz	2 cups
570mL	0 fl oz	
1 litre	35.3 fl oz	4 cups

Length Measures

Metric millimetres (mm), centimetres (cm)	Imperial inches (in), feet (ft)
5mm, 0.5cm	¼ in
10mm, 1.0cm	½ in
20mm, 2.0cm	¾ in
2.5cm	1in
5 cm	2in
7½ cm	3in
10cm	4in
12½ cm	5in
15cm	6in
18cm	7in
20cm	8in
23cm	9in
25cm	10in
28cm	11in
30cm	12in, 1 foot

Index